Against Transgression

Against Transgression

ASHLEY TAUCHERT

WILEY-
BLACKWELL

BLACKWELL PUBLISHING
350 Main Street, Malden, MA 02148-5020, USA
9600 Garsington Road, Oxford OX4 2DQ, UK
550 Swanston Street, Carlton, Victoria 3053, Australia

First published 2008 by Blackwell Publishing Ltd

1 2008

Library of Congress Cataloging-in-Publication Data
Tauchert, Ashley.
Against transgression / Ashley Tauchert.
    p. cm. – (Critical quarterly book series)
  Includes bibliographical references and index.
  ISBN 978-1-4051-6989-9 (alk. paper)
  1. Bataille, Georges, 1897-1962–Criticism and interpretation. I. Title.

PQ2603.A695Z89 2008
848′.91209–dc22

2008001682

A catalogue record for this title is available from the British Library.

Set in 10 on 13 pt Palatino
by Macmillan India
Printed and bound in Singapore
by Fabulous Printers Pte Ltd

For further information on
Blackwell Publishing, visit our website at
www.blackwellpublishing.com

Contents

Acknowledgements

This study would not have been finished on time or in the same mode without the academic labour of Anna Hunt (PhD) as research assistant. The Appendix ('Timeline of Transgression') is entirely her work and her patient contributions of thorough reference materials and intelligent feedback have directly informed the direction of the discussion. I look forward to reading her first book when it comes out...

I am also grateful to Colin as series editor for providing the impetus and public space to think through the problem for feminist maternity that is transgression.

Many thanks to my Department and University for letting me continue to get away with it.

Eternal gratitude and love to my family for making it all worthwhile...

The mother ... she gives rise to all figures by losing herself in the background of the scene like an anonymous persona. Everything comes back to her, beginning with life; everything addresses and destinies itself to her.[1] (Derrida)

Introduction: reflections of a transgressive daughter and her maternal transfiguration

The issue of the relationship between experience and knowledge is still problematic in the liberatory epistemologies. It is important to preserve the integrity and wisdom inherent in culturally specific experiences, and especially in previously ignored and devalued ones, while also coming to terms with the fact that experience in many respects hides the realities of our lives: experience 'lies'. It is necessary to avoid the 'view from nowhere' stance of conventional Western epistemology while refusing to embrace the exaltation of the spontaneous consciousness of our experiences – the experiential foundationalism – that has too often appeared to be the only alternative.[2] (Harding)

Things must be pushed to the limit, where naturally they collapse and are inverted.[3] (Baudrillard)

The unconditional universality of the categorical imperative is evangelical. The moral law inscribes itself at the bottom of our hearts like a memory of the Passion.[4] (Derrida)

A word on the title to begin then. I was reading a submission for *Critical Quarterly*. It passed peaceably over me until all at once I was conscious of a thought I had not had, or noticed, before. The paper argued that, in spite of *surface* appearances, when subjected to *proper* interpretation, author X was fundamentally 'transgressive'. This was the sum point of analysis: to locate and identify points of transgressive thought in the works of author X. It told me neither why transgression was in itself a worthy endeavour, nor why it would bother to secrete itself within the terms of otherwise un-transgressive narratives. The core argument was familiar: I had read it many times in precocious essays by students busy absorbing the increasingly dominant theoretical paradigm of Foucault, or in feminist-identified work (including my own) that sought to celebrate transgression as the impulse toward liberation. I recalled an otherwise intelligent student who had tried to argue that the repressive hypothesis allowed us to reframe paedophilia as a 'repressed' mode of desire. I couldn't quite recall why transgression was a valuable thing to be found, a lost object perpetually uncovered by ever-more-sophisticated forms of analysis, the one thing needful to make an argument worth making. I woke as if from a daydream, woke to the thought of my mother long-since dead. I named the thought: Against Transgression.

The title is a conscious refiguring of Susan Sontag's brilliant essay 'Against Interpretation' and follows the counter-intuitive movement of that argument:

> Thus, interpretation is not (as most people assume) an absolute value, a gesture of mind situated in some timeless realm of capabilities. Interpretation must itself be evaluated, within a historical view of human consciousness. In some cultural contexts, interpretation is a liberating act. It is a means of revising, of transvaluing, of escaping the dead past. In other cultural contexts, it is reactionary, impertinent, cowardly, stifling.
>
> Today is such a time, when the project of interpretation is largely reactionary, stifling. Like the fumes of the automobile and of heavy industry which befoul the urban atmosphere, the effusion of interpretations of art today poisons our sensibilities. In a culture whose already classical dilemma is the hypertrophy of the intellect at the expense of energy and sensual capability, interpretation is the revenge of the intellect upon art . . . Even more. It is the revenge of the intellect upon the world.[5]

I want to consider here the possibility that transgression is not (as some critics assume) an absolute value. Transgression has a history. In some cultural contexts, transgression is a liberating act, a means of revising, transvaluing, escaping a dead past. In the context of the contemporary academy, it is reactionary, impertinent, cowardly, stifling. Like the fumes of the automobile and heavy industry which befoul the atmosphere, transgression poisons our critical sensibilities. In a culture whose classic dilemma is the hypertrophy of the individual will at the expense of a collective energy and capability, transgression is the revenge of the individual ego on the collective unconscious. It is also the revenge of the culturally empowered on the culturally disempowered: an increasingly shrill projection onto those who dare to remain unliberated in the wake of successive waves of radical critique. Why did the revolution not happen? Because some continue to refuse to believe they are oppressed enough to join the revolt. This refusal is tied up with an irrational hope: that things might still turn out for the greater good. Why a thought of my mother? Because this is at least partly a generational argument: Oedipal rage at the father's power is pantomime beyond the growing pains of adolescence. Electra's murderous intentions haunt the daughter when she finds herself becoming a mother in turn.

Yes, this is an oddly personal book. If you are not interested in the relationship between experience and theorizing I would read no further, and I hope you have reached this point before committing any of your own money. This is a book about the changing contextual forces driving my own intellectual development, which may after all only be interesting to me. Sandra Harding's model of 'strong objectivity' invites a reflective critical space in which it seems excusable, if not legitimate, to laugh at the posturing evident in some contemporary critical thought.

The concept of 'strong objectivity' emerges from the philosophy of science, where Harding's feminist epistemology foregrounds the partial perspective of the dominant model of knowledge:

> In an important sense, our cultures have agendas and make assumptions that we as individuals cannot easily detect. Theoretically unmediated experience, that aspect of a group's or an individual's experience in which cultural influences can't be detected, functions as part of the evidence for scientific claims ... we can think of strong objectivity as extending the notion of scientific research to include systematic examination of such powerful background beliefs. It must do so in order to be competent at maximizing objectivity.[6]

While objectivity is not an anxiety for 'the arts' in the same way that it is for 'the sciences', similar problems emerge in relation to the background assumptions shaping largely homogenous communities of knowledge through the Higher Education institutions and research networks that conduct research in literature. Harding's point is that 'starting thought from women's lives' can 'make strange what had appeared familiar' and

> increases the objectivity of the results of research by bringing scientific observations and perception of the need for explanation to bear on assumptions and practices that appear natural or unremarkable from the perspective of the lives of men in the dominant groups.[7]

The thought that is traced through this work initiated in the daily life of a mother who also happens to be a literary theorist.

Pamela Sue Anderson has more recently described Harding's 'strong objectivity' as one of the four 'intellectual virtues' she advocates in her 'epistemological-ethical approach':[8]

> A guiding question for this virtue: are we (and if not, should we be) motivated to bring about strongly objective knowledge?

The other three intellectual virtues she foregrounds for feminist epistemology are *reflexive critical openness, care-knowing,* and *principled autonomy*. 'Strong objectivity' is at one level an attempt to acknowledge the subjectivity of the agent of knowledge in the claim to knowledge:

> In Harding's more recent terms, a 'robust reflexivity' is necessary, if we expect our listening to, and thinking from, the lives of others to transform our weakly objective perspectives. The goal of strong objectivity is, thus, less partial knowledge of our material and social reality, not absolute knowledge.

A 'robust reflexivity' would need to foreground the *immediate* context for any serious claim to knowledge. That context can only ever be partially known as part of an effort to become conscious of the 'objective forces' which shape experience and knowledge. The attempt seems worth the making even if it does also risk narcissism. The personal is, after all, the critical. We look for affirmations of ourselves in the authors and critics we study (otherwise why would we *care* whether T. S. Eliot was anti-semitic as well as a great English poet?) We should also look to be changed in ways unexpected. Only then are we listening for answers previously unheard to persistent questions that seem to be integral to the human condition. This form of listening demands a conscious (one might say romantic) optimism in spite of all the evidence driving us towards a more 'realist' pessimism. Anderson also notes that 'patiently hoping is a virtue when we hope in an *active* sense.'[9] Without hope there is no future worth working towards. On what might we base that hope now?

Between the birth of my son and the break-up of a short and difficult marriage I started out on a PhD thesis about the work of Mary Wollstonecraft. This research became *Accent of the Feminine* (2002). That book – I recently thought, turning it over in my hands – has a weird tone, described quite accurately by one exasperated reviewer as 'dogmatic'. The tone is the residue of a strong chain of experience that left me living the life of a single parent in North London, alone and penniless, with only wine, song and Mary Wollstonecraft to comfort the long, dark evenings (it is always winter in my memory of those days). Her image is before me as I write – literally, as a print of the Opie portrait sits on my writing desk. She looks relaxed, philosophical, dreamy. Something of her voice returns in the pages of this discussion, if you have an ear for it.

Coincidentally, I saw a poster on the door of a prestigious English department office recently that quoted the unacknowledged words of Mary Wollstonecraft beneath a portrait of Mary Shelley: 'I do not wish them [women] to have power over men; but over themselves'. Or at least over their representations. How mothers and daughters entwine, in life as well as in literary history. My written work seems to emerge from a one-sided dialogue with my own mother, Barbara Elizabeth. She died in 1997. That year I passed my Viva, pregnant and without flying colours, then had my third child. Ten years have passed through me since then. I discarded the brittle identity of rebellious daughter some time since. Jane Austen helped me at that stile.

Romancing Jane Austen arose from the new set of critical questions that followed from finding unexpected happiness in a new relationship. I hadn't ever believed that I might *really* fall in love. It was a devastating experience. The theorizing of the grounds for marital despair that conditioned my approach to Wollstonecraft had somehow given way to the theorizing of the possibility of a happy ending (in spite of all the odds) performed with such modest panache by Austen. Everyone desires a happy ending after all. Austen's work provides the narrative blueprint for achieving one under conditions of beautified realism. This blueprint, when abstracted from the particular context for her representations, is what we recognize as romance.

I continue to be intrigued by this interplay between romance as narrative mode and the romantic as a particular mood of desire:

> How eloquent could Anne Elliot have been, – how eloquent, at least, were her wishes on the side of early warm attachment, and a cheerful confidence in futurity, against the over-anxious caution which seems to insult exertion and distrust Providence! – She had been forced into prudence in her youth, she learned romance as she grew older – the natural sequel of an unnatural beginning.[10]

Learning romance means, for Austen, learning to trust 'Providence', to maintain a 'cheerful confidence in futurity': active hoping. Active hoping is difficult under social and intellectual conditions that testify to the final end of hope. All roads lead to death, of the individual and of the species, even of the planet, and – physicists would add – of the universe itself when the sun has finally spent its energy. Everyone living in the world today will not be living one day in the not too distant future. This simple but often overlooked fact is central to the ideas explored in this book.

Looking again at Wollstonecraft in the image before me I can see that she too had learned romance, perhaps too late for her own salvation. Now it's a painful thing, this transitioning from rebellious daughter to 'good enough' mother. If only that were the end of it, but there is more. That experiential transition, day by day, under pressure of an inexorable re-gearing between relative happiness and conditions of increasing constraint, gradually removed the premises on which I had previously justified the unrestrained, transgressive life of a rebellious daughter. Feminist politics *demands* transgression of unjust codes of conduct, because feminist consciousness testifies to conditions of unreasonable constraint: *patriarchal oppression*. The unhappy feminist consciousness finds the source of its unhappiness in the discord between female-embodied subjectivity and its objective context. Transgression has an important role as a direct expression of this discord, but it is not enough in itself to resolve it. If we decided to practise 'active hope' in our work, we would need to move away from a preoccupation with expression towards a determination to resolve. My argument here, for what it's worth, is that this move can be initiated by a conscious shift from focusing on transgression to focusing on compassion. It will take some time to unfold this argument and I am entirely dependent on your patience for its understanding. I will try to keep the journey as short and interesting as possible.

Good-enough mothers may continue to practise middle-aged modifications of their daughterly rebellions, but on reflection they should find that they no longer have the grounds or the right to *preach* transgression. After all, what would happen to the daughter's right to transgress if the mother remained an agent of transgression? Wollstonecraft, that exemplary transgressive mother, had this thought on the evening before leaving her infant daughter for the first time:

> You know that as a mother I am particularly attached to her – I feel more than a mother's fondness and anxiety, when I reflect on the dependent and oppressed state of her sex. I dread lest she should be forced to sacrifice her heart to her principles, or principles to her heart. With trembling hand I shall cultivate sensibility, and cherish delicacy of sentiment, lest, whilst I lend fresh blushes to the rose, I sharpen the thorns that will wound the breast I would fain guard – I dread to unfold her mind, lest it should render her unfit for the world she is to inhabit – Haplass woman! what a fate is thine![11]

This is Wollstonecraft pining for her daughter's father, that infamous feminist anti-hero; Gilbert Imlay. Her maternal reflection carries traces of her own approaching fate as she felt him recede from their life together, facing the uncertain future of an unmarried mother without even the minimal support of a welfare state. This haunting fear for her daughter's future is also expressed as a romantic longing for a simple domesticity:

> It was Saturday, and the evening was uncommonly serene. In the villages every where I saw preparations for Sunday; and I passed by a little car loaded with rye, that presented, for the pencil and heart, the sweetest picture of a harvest home I had ever beheld! A little girl was mounted a straddle on a shaggy horse, brandishing a stick over its head; the father was walking at the side of the car with a child in his arms, who must have come to meet him with tottering steps, the little creature was stretching out its arms to cling around his neck; and a boy, just above petticoats, was labouring hard, with a fork, behind, to keep the sheaves from falling.
>
> My eyes followed them to the cottage, and an involuntary sigh whispered to my heart, that I envied the mother, much as I dislike cooking, who was preparing their pottage.[12]

This is late Wollstonecraft. She died only a couple of years after writing it, not long after the birth of her second daughter, by then married to the famous rational philosopher, William Godwin. Her motherless daughters' subsequent fates are now well-documented. She had very good reason to be concerned about their futures. Fanny (the babe she writes about so powerfully during her journey through Scandinavia) committed suicide in 1816. Janet Todd describes the chilling circumstances of Fanny's death well:

> She dressed herself in her mother's stays [initialled M.W.] and took with her the gold watch Mary [Shelley] had brought her from Switzerland, a red pocket handkerchief, a brown berry necklace and a small leather purse.[13]

Her body was never claimed by her family and she was buried in a pauper's grave. Her suicide note (with the signature torn off) reads:

> I have long determined that the best thing I could do was to put an end to the existence of a being whose birth was unfortunate, and whose life has only been a series of pain to those persons who have hurt their health in endeavouring to promote her welfare. Perhaps to hear of my death will give you pain, but you will soon have the blessing of forgetting that such a creature ever existed as ...[14]

Her more famous second daughter, Mary (Wollstonecraft Godwin) Shelley, had already eloped with the atheist poet dedicated to a life of free love; she was regularly pregnant from age 16 or in mourning for one of her babies. His first wife (Harriet Westbrook, also 16 when they eloped) committed suicide, also in 1816, pregnant with her third child (possibly Shelley's according to Janet Todd's recent study). Mary's father, William Godwin, had been a strong advocate of atheism and its concomitant, free love, in his younger days; yet he never seems to have forgiven Shelley or his daughter for attempting to live out these ideals. Free love, or sexual liberation, is always mixed up with transgression as a critical thought.

Free love has remained a preoccupation of liberatory movements since the 1790s, most recently manifesting openly in post-1960s Western Europe. I was born into the middle of 1960s London, but was not a by-product of free love. The 'sexual revolution' was complete before I became conscious of sexuality. Life for women prior to the collective transgressions of the mid-1960s is now unimaginable:

> until the mid-1960s it was virtually impossible for a single woman to furnish herself with birth control … in some British family planning clinics, where contraception would be prescribed to the engaged, the receipt for the wedding dress was required as proof that the applicant was free from intentions of immorality … until the licensing of the Pill in 1960, it was men who took charge of contraception … landlords would not rent to unmarried couples … abortion and homosexuality were illegal and the divorce laws trapped people in violent or loveless marriages … there was no sexual persona for the post-nubile single woman …[15]

It may now be the case that there is no longer an accessible non-sexual persona for women. However, as Grant goes on to consider, '[i]f there had been a sexual revolution, why did women still fear rape whenever they stepped outside their house' and '*why* had female desire not transformed the world?'[16] The 'sexual revolution' promised a future of uninhibited sexual expression as the core means to the transformation of society. The ensuing reality has turned out to be more complicated than that.

Sheila Jeffereys underlined the strong contradictions at work in the Western sexual revolution of the 20th century:

> The sexual revolution was heterosexual … Sexual liberals like the Hegelers tried hard to be non-judgmental about homosexuality and devoted a good few pages to the issue in the *ABZ of Love*. They saw homosexuals as worthy of tolerant understanding and as having the right to a sexual life. It would have been difficult to take a different line when they were liberal about everything else from paedophilia to necrophilia. But Alex Comfort, self-proclaimed sex radical, remained unaffected by this liberal urge, though he too waxed enthusiastic about group sex, anal sex and many other activities which carried serious taboos. He claimed to cover all varieties of sexual behaviour in *The Joy of Sex* but did not include homosexuality …[17]

The dream of a sexual revolution has not been realized, or has been foreclosed, so long as our experience and understanding of human sexuality remains limited to a 'natural' heterosexual dyad. But it is not clear to me that this would mean that human sexuality could be imagined without limits. Those limits are related to the moral basis of human societies, in the form of foundational prohibitions or 'taboos'. The heterosexual dyad, and its specific dynamic of productive sexual difference, does have a strong claim to be acknowledged as a foundational unit of human creation and survival. There have been many worthy experiments with collective living beyond the family, but the heterosexual dyad still remains at the core of human creativity and survival as embodiment of the irreducible basis of conception in sexual difference. We have enjoyed important changes to the law in response to mass transgressions of normative social and sexual relations, including decriminalization of male homosexuality. The idea I am approaching through the following chapters can best be understood through the thought that recognition of these rights bring us *closer to* – rather than *further from* – realizing a universal moral law.

How to realize the desire for sexual liberation without losing the subtle and clearly fragile forms of bonding that constitute the complex interweave of a good-enough life? Sexual liberation in general terms is the sexualization of desire for a free society, an identification of sexual repression with the more comprehensive oppression of human creative potential. Transgression goes further, seeking out the secret modes of regularity that structure human life and consciousness *by breaching their terms*. Georges Bataille, a key figure in the intellectual genealogy of transgression and a core subject of this book, found its essential manifestation in the late 18th-century writings of the Marquis de Sade:

> what de Sade was trying to bring to the surface of the conscious mind was precisely the thing that revolted that mind. For him the most revolting thing was the most powerful means of exciting pleasure. Not only did he reach the most singular revelations by these means, but from the very first he set before the consciousness, things which it could not tolerate. He himself spoke only of 'irregularity'. The rules we obey are usually intended to conserve life; hence irregularity leads towards destruction ... De Sade knew nothing about the basic interrelation of taboo and transgression, opposite and complementary concepts. But he took the first step. This general mechanism could not be completely comprehended until we finally and tardily arrived at an understanding of the paradox of taboo and transgression.[18]

The productive irregularity which is the experience of transgression can only be experienced once regularities are firmly in place. De Sade was writing in the midst of revolutionary excess, his writings perform at a literary level the action that at a social level concretized itself in the act of killing the King. De Sade's transgression in writing manifested the context for that writing in some startlingly clear ways: his preferred model of liberation was an expression of sovereignty, the masterful individual enjoying an absolute will which objectifies the other to the point of death. Adorno noted that Sade's 'private vice constitutes a predictive chronicle of the public virtues of the totalitarian era.'[19]

> Not to have glossed over or suppressed but to have trumpeted far and wide the impossibility of deriving from reason any fundamental argument against murder fired the hatred which the progressives (and they precisely) still direct against Sade and Nietzsche.

As an immanent critique of the myth of Enlightenment, Bataille and his intellectual ancestors (Sade and Nietzsche) cut like razors. As a recommended item on a reading list for an undergraduate module teaching 'Transgression', Sade's works represent a kind of failure of confidence in the intellectual autonomy of the next generation. There is something creepy about the tendency towards introducing texts of transgression to our students; particularly the way these have crept into syllabi alongside a modularization that rests on the marketing of modules and programmes.

Where does this leave critical transgression? Exactly where it has been for some time, between the pages of a book on a number of academic reading lists. It is interesting to 'google' through the range of advanced Higher Education credit-bearing modules containing the word 'Transgression' with carefully formulated 'learning outcomes' and 'assessment' models. Satisfactory completion of a module on 'Taboo' is apparently not a prerequisite to the study of 'Transgression'. In the diversity of critical and cultural activity through which this concept is now promoted, a stifling uniformity is emerging. Transgression has become a critical virtue, signifying freedom and the end of oppression. Yet the student who chooses to transgress an educational climate that now increasingly promotes the *concept of* transgression faces a penalty. The objective power of the institutions in and through which the concept of a virtuous transgression is constructed and distributed is important. Transgression has become a safe topic for the progressive intellectual. At the same time, transgression as a critical concept nestles comfortably within, is promoted by and reinforces, increasingly regulatory educational structures.

I have come to understand that it is not possible for me to think through the claims of transgression without referring to my experience as a mother or, to put it in more theoretical terms, a *maternal subject*. The history of the thought of transgression is littered with the bodies of raped and murdered mothers. Kathy Acker saw the figure of the mother as central to de Sade's philosophy:

> By the end of the seventh dialogue, Eugénie has been seduced. In fact it took no time at all, ten or twelve pages, for the scoundrelly adults to rob the poor child of her virginity, Sade-style, in the ass. But true virginity, for the Marquis, is not physical. It takes the monsters of corruption more than 150 pages to teach Eugénie that she can do whatever she pleases: fuck and get fucked in every possible way, blaspheme God, . . . disobey, fuck and sew up her mother's cunt to ensure that her mother will no longer interfere in Eugénie's affairs.[20]

Mothers are the primal scene of transgression: 'women who . . . want their freedom, hate their mothers. In de Sade's texts, mothers are prudes, haters of their own bodies, and religious fanatics, for they are obedient to the tenets of a patriarchal society. The daughter who does not reject her mother interiorizes prison.'[21] Freedom for the daughter is premised on rejection of the mother, or at least the mother's embodiment of a 'repressive' normativity that seems to refute sexuality and liberty in favour of prohibition and restraint. Transgressive feminism might be said to have foregrounded the concerns of daughters over mothers.

Furthermore, maternal subjectivity as such is an anomaly in critical thought. Can the *Mother* speak? For Julia Kristeva, as Elizabeth Grosz has demonstrated, maternal subjectivity remains structurally non-existent:

> Kristeva claims that maternity is the unspoken foundation of social and signifying relations, the 'origin' of heterogeneity and archaic jouissance, the source of the child's corporeal organization and the object to which its desires are directed. Maternity, however, remains strictly outside symbolization – ideally it is repressed or sublimated in order that unity, stability, identity and a speaking position for the child is possible. Yet, ironically, in Kristeva's work, women have no special link to the maternal body, either as a specifically female child who takes up her position in relation to the maternal body . . . or in her position as a mother . . . The female is paradoxically precluded from representing or speaking maternity and femininity.[22]

Iris Young did however make an interesting attempt to articulate pregnant subjectivity, following Kristeva's notion that '[pregnancy] seems to be experienced as the radical ordeal of the splitting of the subject: redoubling up of the body, separation and coexistence of the self and an other, of nature and consciousness, of physiology and speech'.[23] Young writes in the pregnant first-person, foregrounding the experience of pregnancy as the point of departure for an articulation of maternity:

> Pregnancy challenges the integration of my body experience by rendering fluid the boundary between what is within, myself, and what is outside, separate. I experience my insides as the space of another, yet my own body.[24]

A maternal subject, then, experiences first-hand the gradual formation of the embodied subject that she is involved in creating. Following birth, she (or care-providers in her place) provides and reinforces patterns of sustainable regularity (bodily and psychic) for the emergent consciousness of the child. Such basic and uninteresting order is intrinsic to human survival: the processing of faeces, regulation of the ingestion of food, the (often ritual) cleansing of the body, temporal order relating the child's behaviour to the cycle of day and night and the seasons, socially appropriate use of clothing, early ordering of language games into purposive communication, repression of some of the child's animalistic desires to ensure relatively peaceful social relations in a human society. Primary morality is the sum of repetitive activities aimed at ensuring the survival and wellbeing of the child in the short and longer term according to inherited, and culturally modified, principles. The child's experience of the regulation of her drives, however, involves constant frustration and redirection of her emergent desires. This is prohibition as an elementary factor in human survival.[25]

Partly this is a generational argument, both at the personal and the critical levels. A maternal subject must regulate her own desires in order to teach regularity to her children. She learns, through an experience of love, to order herself differently. Her daughters will probably learn her lesson over time, but the process is conflicted and denied transcendence by the absence of cultural forms for female-female inheritance:

> Female to female inheritance has, of course, always been problematic in a patriarchal society in which the legacy passed from male to male is

understood as natural and of central importance. Even today men can be unselfconsciously honoured as the fathers of artistic movements, scientific fields, inventions, ideas. Advances in thought are reified into systems by being named for their male founders: so we have Marxism, Freudianism, Darwinism. It is no accident that feminism was not named after an individual woman. If, sometimes, a mother for feminism is mooted – Mary Wollstonecraft, for example – it is always tentatively, with irony, or in the spirit of daughterly insurrection . . . In a patriarchal society the mother's role of subordination and self-sacrifice is what the daughter does not want to inherit.[26]

The articulation of a *critical* maternal subjectivity, then, might also be concerned with engendering regularity and sustainability in the other: working at the possibility for creating and reinforcing forms of productive female-embodied agency; in writing, in narrative, in professional conduct, in theory, in practice, in our students. Critical maternal subjectivity might just have something interesting to say about transgression.

I have recently come to understand agency differently from the way I did as a transgressive daughter. Freedom and necessity (constraint) have turned out to be entwined in ways it was not possible to discover by critical theory alone, however committed and ethical the project understands itself to be. Preaching transgression from a position of authority might suggest that regularity itself has been overturned in the name of liberation, but the fact remains that any *experience* of transgression depends on the regulation of human conduct.

In the first chapter I follow the thought of transgression through Bataille and his post-structural mediation by Foucault into the field of contemporary critical thought. I open a discussion here of the peculiar place of female-embodiment in Bataille's model of transgression. Women are central to contemporary transgression's genealogy: Marie-Antoinette Bataille (Bataille's mother) and Colette Peignot ('Laure') in particular. Chapter two turns to consider the particular experience of female-embodied transgression through a disorienting encounter with *Story of O*. In this section I speculate on the question of agency under constraint as a condition of the feminine subject. *O* offers the key to a highly feminine mode of transgression centred on the possibility of transcendence through constraint (rather than liberation). This discussion raises the odd but important question of a relationship between femininity and the 'sacred'. In the third chapter I consider Bataille's work in relation to his historical antithesis: the Anglo-Irish Christian fantasist, C.S. Lewis. The sacred is addressed directly by both thinkers, since both are writing at least partly in response to an encounter with Nietzsche. Lewis offers a refreshingly different and challenging set of answers to the critical questions also faced by Bataille, and I want to use this odd contrast to make us think clearly about this very particular model of thought and its phenomenal influence on critical work today. The last chapter is in the form of a preface to 'Compassion' over 'Transgression'. The compassion I want to mobilize as a critical virtue is rooted in the concept of 'emptiness' drawn down from Mahayana Buddhist theory. Aspects of 'emptiness awareness' are already evident in late Western thought, from Irigarayan feminist theology to CR. 'Emptiness' is arguably synonymous with the condition of 'continuity' that is glimpsed through Bataillean transgression. I argue here, however, that the kind of 'emptiness awareness' seeping into contemporary critical thought is inadequate to the goal of liberation without the active and importantly related practice of 'compassion'. The Buddhist theory of 'emptiness' emerges from acknowledgment of all others *as if* they were your living mother. This conscious return to a living maternal subject as the object of compassion in the face of emptiness offers an intriguing alternative to a critical model of transgression which seems to twist itself compulsively around the figure of a dead mother's body.

1

Preface Against Transgression: Bataillean 'Transgression' and its colonization of contemporary critical thought

If there is a single term poststructuralism could not live without . . . it is 'transgression,' inherited from Bataille . . . Foucault established transgression as an alternative to the machine of dialectical contradiction.[27] (Guerlac)

In his insistence that sex is intimately connected to death and that this connection is the fundamental force which animates our religious feelings, Bataille remains a thinker whose full impact has yet to be measured. But if his thought is to be developed then there can be little doubt that it will need a very considerable engagement with feminism . . . one might well question whether the entire structure of his thought from the place of death to that of expenditure is a fundamentally masculine one.[28] (MacCabe)

'I guess what you want to see is the old rag and ruin,' she said. Hanging on to the tabletop with both hands, I twisted around toward her. She was seated, she held one long leg stuck up in the air, to open her crack yet wider she used fingers to draw the folds of skin apart. And so Madame Edwarda's 'old rag and ruin' loured at me, hairy and pink, just as full of life as some loathsome squid. 'Why', I stammered in a subdued tone, 'why are you doing that?' 'You can see for yourself', she said, 'I'm GOD'.[29] (Bataille)

In geology, 'transgression' is the migration of a shoreline out of an oceanic basin and onto land: the colonization of the land by the sea. Geological transgression takes place when conditions for the boundary line between land and sea change, testifying both to the inevitability of the boundary line and to its final instability. Transgression occurs when the border between land and sea is erased at the expense of the land. What was the limit of the solid ground for human habitation and culture gives way to the fluid forces of the oceanic. Footprints are erased and sandcastles washed away. The antonym of a geological transgression is 'regression', where the shoreline extends itself as the sea recedes. There's something in the geological figure of trangression that resonates with the intellectual anxiety at work in the proliferation of the term in critical work since the 1960s. Critical transgression is characterized by an underlying philosophy of excess and anguish, overspilling of boundaries, breaking of taboos, denaturalizing of cultural codes of order. Transgression in both cases marks the breaking of a boundary; understood in critical humanism as 'taboo'. If the only alternative to the transgressive tide in our thinking practices is indeed regression, then the compulsion to go further, find ever new boundaries to breach, may be motivated by an anxiety of annihilation by a past that would quite simply not have tolerated us as we have come to be. We seek transgression to ward off fear of regression. If transgression is the limit, however, when does the tide turn towards regression? We are caught between the twin polarities of repression. According to Judith Butler, there are two primary taboos ordering the shape of gendered human consciousness: homosexuality and incest. We face the question of their covalence.[30]

It is impossible to consider seriously the place of transgression in contemporary academic thought without considering seriously the work of Georges Bataille. I have long avoided considering at any level the work of Georges Bataille since reading *Story of the Eye* (1928) many years ago and finding it neither exciting nor particularly interesting except as a kind of desperate, failed pornography that offered images for which I had no response. Eggs and bulls' testicles and exorbitated eyes do nothing for me and I turned away in bemused indignation. This book will not be a study of that notorious anti-novel, except insofar as I am interested in the forces that produced its extraordinary preoccupations, and that continue to draw a body of critical thought to its knees before the master of transgression.

Bataille opened a serious and largely undigested discussion of the 'cohesion of the human spirit' that is compelling and remains to be fully answered. His study of *Eroticism* (1957) is a fascinating attempt to show this cohesion; one which can accommodate both the ascetic and the voluptuary, the saint and the sinner, grace and dissolution, pure spirit and base matter. This is arguably *not* the aspect of Bataille's thought mediated by Michel Foucault's influential 'Preface to Transgression' in 1963. Bataille's work illuminated in his own inimitable way a profound and fundamentally irrational continuity between the transgressor and the saint: a figure of debased female prostitution embodies his 'GOD'. Foucault's account of Bataille, inherited and proliferated by contemporary critical thought, seems to return compulsively towards the addictive thrill of a thought of transgression in the name of a final liberation from humanity itself. Like a child at the sea-shore putting in a toe and enjoying the feel of the cold water, then jumping back in fear when splashed by a breaking wave.

Let's begin with Bataille's most fundamental statement, which is repeated in a bewilderment of different forms throughout his theoretical works:

> We are discontinuous beings, individuals who perish in isolation in the midst of an incomprehensible adventure, but we yearn for our lost continuity. We find the state of affairs that binds us to our random and ephemeral individuality hard to bear. Along with our tormenting desire that this evanescent thing should last, there stands our obsession with a primal continuity linking us with everything that is . . . this nostalgia is responsible for the three forms of eroticism in man.[31]

I am particularly interested in Bataille's ideas of continuity and discontinuity and their relation to the contemporary critical preoccupation with transgressive desires and theoretical eroticism. Bataille's language of 'continuity' and 'discontinuity' defamiliarizes the religious signifiers traditionally deployed to think through these questions: he 'thought it better to be less easily understood and more accurate.'[32] 'Continuity' can be folded back into Christian ideas of 'eternity' or 'salvation', but it can also refer out to recognition of 'emptiness' in the Buddhist tradition.

The intellectual engagement with questions of the final truth of human consciousness initiated by Bataille has been subsequently reified into a commodified critical desire to identify with the anguished and transgressive itself; a desire that has come to operate an unconscious fascination for academic thought, all the more compulsive as it is unconscious. By making the conditions of this thought conscious we can face it and decide what is to be done with it. Unconsciously motivated thought cannot be socially responsible thought, and we would do well to remember our responsibilities to each other and to the younger generation of thinkers. So this is also a book about power, the power of thought, and the power to generate and direct thought. The final concern of this work is to begin a process of understanding how it is that academic theorists can be so excited by transgressive thoughts, but dismayed by the effects of transgression in the social world.[33] It is all very well and good to celebrate Bataille's condensed image of the exorbitated eye: quite another thing to have one's own eyes exorbitated. If this sounds naïve I am happy for it to be so, since to turn away from the fascinated, morbid play of critical transgression is finally to turn towards a conscious innocence that might just be more powerful in the end.

Denis Hollier argues that Bataille's 'transgression is a transgression of form'.[34] The dialectical exchange between land and sea that borders human life and consciousness continually works at the dividing line between conditions of form and formlessness. Form is a semi-permanent feature of the material landscape; the ceaseless pulsions of the ocean work to dissolve the solidity of material form. Inestimably dense rock turns eventually to sand, cliff faces are eroded; material forms dispersed by the formless fluidity of the oceanic. In Hollier's account, Bataille's work, by 'juxtapos[ing] fiction and theory in a way that destroys sublimation', exposes and collapses 'the separation of knowledge and sexual pleasure'.[35] If 'knowledge' stands for the calcified forms of human consciousness, and 'sexual pleasure' for the unknowable forces that ceaselessly motivate and undermine human endeavour, Bataille's intellectual transgressions might be as refreshing to witness as the ceaseless breaking of waves on the impassive shoreline. However, transgression of form also makes me think of cancer.

Anthony Julius has recently outlined the history of transgression in Western art. His impressive study of *Transgressions: The Offences of Art* (2002) shows how 'the transgressive' is 'among other things, a determinate aesthetic, one that promoted the making of artworks of a certain kind during the modern period', a potential that now seems to have been 'exhausted' in the Western tradition.[36] His working definition of transgression exposes its 'founding tension':

> There is a primary, theological sense of transgression. It is a sin, a super-crime, an offence against God. In Milton's *Paradise Lost*, for example, Adam and Eve 'transgress [God's] will' when they eat the forbidden fruit ... The negative charge of this meaning is complicated in its usage by a certain antinomianism, a positive celebration of law-breaking. It is by our law-breaking that we disclose our state of grace. One finds this meaning in St. Paul. So there is a founding tension. Transgressions are both the best and worse kind of law-breaking, which can perhaps be compressed thus: transgressions are outrages that can liberate.[37]

Julius traces the history of transgression as a word which 'entered the English language in the 16th century freighted with these negative scriptural meanings' and was 'soon secularised to describe disobedience of the law'. He notes that the 'concept of the "transgressive" lives its real life in contemporary cultural discourse, where it is highly regarded and much deployed':

> To describe an artwork as 'transgressive' is to offer it a compliment . . . It is successor to the Romantic ideology of the artist as genius, a rule-breaker indifferent to art's constraints. [. . .] The transgressive also has a certain political flavour, opposing the stereotypical and the self-enclosed, and generating the 'open' and the 'hybrid' . . . Boundaries are to be deprecated; they resonate with everything that is petrified, stale, encrusted, immobile. Boundary-breaking is to be admired; it resonates with everything that is fluid, fresh, unencumbered, mobile – and 'cool'.[38]

If we are prepared now to historicize transgression, we must also be ready to personalize it. To personalize Bataille's particular preoccupations (André Breton called him 'obsessional') is not difficult. MacCabe has already noted that the paradigm of transgression Bataille catalysed is peculiarly 'masculine'. He can only really testify to a transgression experienced and expressed through a particular model of excessive expenditure that conforms to the hydraulics of male orgasm (the intellectual outcome of a life 'spent' in brothels perhaps). On the other hand, the one with which I am inevitably more familiar, Bataille's transgression captures a very intimate and highly charged encounter with some extraordinary figures of female-embodied subjectivity. When we think through the implications of transgression from their 'stand point' we approach a central association between femininity and the sacred. This is an interesting conjunction to find skulking in the shadows of contemporary critical thought.

Finally, Julius's summary of Bataille's critical footprint is exemplary and worth considering in full before we go any further:

> [Bataille] argues as follows. We need to work to detach ourselves from our animal existence; work makes us what we are. Anything that interferes with productive labour risks returning us to that state and therefore cannot be permitted. It is 'taboo'. However, while work liberates us from one form of subordination, it subjects us to another form. We become caught up in an endless labour of production. And so we need, from time to time, to free ourselves from the means of our liberation. Hence the need for the transgression of taboo. This transgression is both a return to an animal existence, where labour is unknown, and an assertion of sovereignty over communal life, where labour is mandatory. We become conscious of ourselves as subjects through work; our consciousness of ourselves as subjects impels us to resist subordination to work. Subjectivity is discovered in work, but expresses itself against work. Transgression thus represents a desire both

for the sovereignty of subjectivity and the extinction of subjectivity – a desire to return to the world from which, through the discovery of subjectivity, man has become separated.[39]

He concludes, rather beautifully, that transgression for Bataille is 'an assertion of dominion combined with a kind of chthonic nostalgia . . . accompanied by the expression of a certain anguish'.

I only want to add that the marked fascination with transgression that has permeated and directed the critical work of a generation (or two) of intellectual labourers might in fact signify a creeping instrumentalization and petrification of critical thought. Perhaps we are drawn to transgression because it allows us to think, at least momentarily, that critical thought itself might still be free. The stultifying thought of transgression screens a longing for the transgression of thought that is called for in its place. The problem that we face is that transgression as an academic concept can of course do nothing to resist the final instrumentalization of critical thought. Critical transgression accommodates itself perfectly to the ever-diminishing, increasingly hollow spaces available to critical thought. Critical transgression, on reflection, can only really express the forces of a very late capitalism in direct (and arguably deadly) encounter with the academy.

Let's consider Bataille's signature scene of representation: the upturned eye, rolling in exctasy or anguish, blindly registering the absence of sight by becoming an obscenely discrete object of sight. The eye violently disgorged from its privileged place belongs ultimately to the figure of the priest who dies in the midst of the last orgy of extreme sexual violence experienced by the vicarious narrator of *Story of the Eye*. In a scene of unsurpassable obscenity, the eye, now removed from the dead priest's body, is spectacularly inserted by Simone into her own sex. The narrator, looking between Simone's legs, sees the blue eye of the priest weeping at him, framed by her vulvic lips:

> Now I stood up and, while Simone lay on her side, I drew her thighs apart, and found myself facing something I imagine I had been waiting for in the same way that a guillotine waits for a neck to slice. I even felt as if my eyes were bulging from my head, erectile with horror; in Simone's hairy vagina, I saw the wan blue eye . . . gazing at me through tears of urine. Streaks of come in the streaming hair helped to give that dreamy vision a disastrous sadness.[40]

It's a uniquely queasy, otherwise unimaginable image; one that I defy anyone to read closely without involuntarily recoiling. Close reading is, incidentally, one of the things I have found difficult in the course of this project.

Foucault famously transformed this obscenely roving, sightless eye into a strong philosophical claim in his inaugural essay of post-structuralist transgression ('Preface to transgression') written to mark Bataille's death in 1963:

> But perhaps the eye accomplishes the most essential aspect of its play when, forced from its ordinary position, it is made to turn upwards in a movement that leads it back to the nocturnal and starred interior of the skull and it is made to show us its usually concealed surface, white and unseeing: it shuts out the day in a movement that manifests its own whiteness ... The upturned orb suggests both the most open and the most impenetrable eye: causing its sphere to pivot, while remaining exactly the same and in the same place where the pupil once opened is like the being of the eye as it crosses the limit of its vision – when it transgresses this opening to the light of day which defined the transgression of every sight ... The upturned eye discovers the bond that links language and death at the moment that it acts out this relationship of the limit and being; and it is perhaps from this that it derives its prestige, in permitting the possibility of a language for this play. Thus, the great scenes that interrupt Bataille's stories invariably concern the spectacle of erotic deaths, where upturned eyes display their white limits and rotate inwards in gigantic and empty orbits.[41]

Speaking frankly, I do find something distasteful in the now common celebration of scenes of violent eroticism. If only this were a *theoretical* concern, but such acts are really not that uncommon in the social world. Not that Bataille's novellas are responsible for the unavoidable human tendency towards murderous violence. Bataille's ability to reveal in representation the shape of an unconscious wish for sexual violence, and its obsessive tendency to sacrifice its objects to an inexplicably ferocious desire, is deeply impressive. It is the work of a thinker who knew more than most the difference between imaginary representation and other kinds of personally and socially transformative action (while diligently practising all of these).

He is particularly good on death:

> Apart from the precarious and random luck that makes possession of the loved one possible, humanity has from the earliest times endeavoured to reach this liberating continuity by means not dependent on chance. The problem arises when man is faced with death which seems to pitch the discontinuous creature headlong into continuity. This way of seeing the matter is not the first that springs to mind, yet death, in that it destroys the discontinuous being, leaves intact the general continuity of existence outside ourselves ... This I think is the way to interpret religious sacrifices, with which I suggest that erotic activity can be compared.

Erotic activity, by dissolving the separate beings that participate in it, reveals their fundamental continuity, like the waves of a stormy sea. In sacrifice, the victim is divested not only of clothes but of life (or is destroyed in some way if it is an inanimate object). The victim dies and the spectators share in what his death reveals. This is what religious historians call the element of sacredness. This sacredness is the revelation of continuity through the death of a discontinuous being to those who watch it as a solemn rite. A violent death disrupts the creature's discontinuity; what remains, what the tense onlookers experience in the succeeding silence, is the continuity of all existence with which the victim is now one. Only a spectacular killing, carried out as the solemn and collective nature of religious dictates, has the power to reveal what normally escapes notice.[42]

There is a serious anecdote that Bataille went so far as to plan to act out this final transgression: the sacrifice of the love object. According to the stories, he had secured the agreement of his lover (Colette Peignot) to be the object of a ritual sacrifice as the inauguration of a new 'Acéphalic' religion, before conceding that neither he nor anyone else would really agree to perform the act. Bataille's biographer, Michel Surya, dismisses the notion, as he does the equally disturbing suggestion that Bataille's pre-war writings reveal a morbid fascination with fascism. Bataille's fascination produced an incisive analysis of fascism:

an organized understanding of the movements in society, of attraction and repulsion, starkly presents itself as a weapon at this moment [1933– 4] when a vast convulsion opposes, not so much fascism to communism, but radical imperative forms to the deep subversion which continues to pursue the emancipation of human lives.[43]

Bataille's aim in his study of 'The Psychological Structure of Fascism', carried forward in the otherwise inexplicable Acephalic rituals, was to found a more powerful cultural mythology than the one mediated to devastating effects by European fascists:

Fascism is a perverted and nostalgic form, but it responds to a deep yearning for a meaningful experience of the sacred ... the success of fascism raised issues that socialism had to address ... What was needed, for Bataille, was the development of a sacred of the left hand that would counter the sacred of the right hand that facism invoked. More than half a century later, this is a question that has barely even been delineated ...[44]

Kathy Acker understands 'Acéphale' as an approach towards 'nonpatriarchal language' by Bataille:

Acéphale's center is the colon; the colon is labyrinthine. In a labyrinth, reason is useless, lost. In the labyrinth, remember Borge's labyrinths, the self becomes lost. In the labyrinth, paths, ways of knowing, seem subject to chance. Chance or Fortune and chaos are simply those lands which lie outside and beyond our understanding.[45]

For Bataille it would only ever be by working at the level of the irrational constellation of forces that allowed fascism to capture and distort 'radical imperative forms', and not at the level of a stupefyingly rational democracy or communism, that its tendencies could be subverted. The '[r]adical imperative forms' he mentions here are important to Bataille's sense of what it is to be human: and the 'emancipation of human lives' is the final object of his wild analysis, associated with the liberation of these radical imperatives and the related possibility of a fully human experience of totality, articulated as the 'suspension of non-continuity'.

Colette Peignot died naturally of tuberculosis. Bataille mourned her death in recognizably human ways, in spite of denying her Catholic mother the comfort of a priest:

> Then death came on 7 November 1938 at 8.15 in the morning. Bataille blamed himself for having fled in the same way he had fled his father's death. He scattered pages of William Blake's poem *The Marriage of Heaven and Hell* into the catafalque over the dead woman's body. 'I will not say how her death came, although the necessity to speak of it exists within me in the most "terrible" way.' He never spoke of it.[46]

The preoccupation with sacrifice, moreover, is a central feature of the landscape of Bataillean thought; but it is never sacrifice for its own sake, or for the sheer excitement available from the thought. Sacrifice is the only basis of community (as shared communion with the sacred) in his analysis of what it is to be human: a collective acknowledgement of the general 'solar' economy of expenditure against which human form is a temporary and finally unsustainable resistance:

> I will begin with a basic fact: the living organism, in a situation determined by the play of energy on the surface of the globe, ordinarily receives more energy than is necessary for maintaining life; the excess energy (wealth) can be used for the growth of a system (eg., an organism); if the system can no longer grow, or if the excess cannot be completely absorbed in its growth, it must necessarily be lost without profit; it must be spent, willingly or not, gloriously or catastrophically.[47]

Sacrifice is at work in Bataille's narrative erotica, and displaced there onto the non-productive sexual acts that dominate his imaginary work:

> We know the ancients identified, at least in poetry, the possession of a
> woman with sacrifice ... women were treated in this instance like
> sacrificial animals. Here I must stress that woman, more than man, is the
> centre of eroticism. She alone is able to devote herself to it, provided she
> doesn't have children in her care. Whereas man is nearly always
> a working or warring animal first of all. However, I have spoken of
> eroticism mainly in reference to man. I did not think it necessary to
> examine each of the situations I have spoken of from a woman's point of
> view. I was less anxious to fully describe the different aspects of
> eroticism than to grasp the movement whereby human existence
> encounters totality in eroticism.[48]

Sexual possession 'of a woman' equals sacrifice in Bataille's symbolic
equation: the one commonly attainable experience of the sacred in a
profane world; perhaps the only experience of the sacred remaining
under the profane conditions of life in post-war Europe. The female
prostitute really is as close as he can get to 'GOD': reviled, outcast,
debased but always and still available (for a price) after dark. This
presents us with the sheer negative of Keats's 'Grecian Urn'. There, the
eternally promised but never fulfilled 'sacrifice' of the 'lowing heifer'
parallels the youth's 'panting' after the 'maidens overwrought' in
one extraordinarily condensed image of the 'wild ecstasy' as 'cold
pastoral'. Bataille's aesthetic inhabits by contrast the 'human passion
... That leaves a heart high-sorrowful and cloy'd'.[49]

This is what, for Bataille, makes base sexual encounters equivalent
to the sacred. This also constitutes Bataillean transgression of thought.
It is, however, not what carries over into contemporary critical forms
of transgression. The very idea of 'the sacred' now seems to have
become the most debased of serious critical thoughts. A.C. Grayling
recently identified any form of religious belief with educational
'dumbing down':

> a significant proportion of university entrants today are noticeably
> different from their average forerunners of a generation ago: measurably
> less literate, less numerate, less broadly knowledgeable, and sometimes
> less reflective. At the same time education has been infected by post-
> modern relativism and the less desirable elements of 'political correct-
> ness', whose combined effect is to encourage teachers to accept, and
> even promote as valid alternatives, the various superstitions and antique
> belief systems constituting the multiplicity of different and generally
> competing religions represented in our multi-cultural society.[50]

That larger percentage of the population who have not come close to a
university – except perhaps as cleaners, porters, shop staff – are given
shorter shrift:

the great mass of religious folk believe in something far more basic and traditional ... into most of whom supernaturalistic beliefs and superstitions were inculcated as children when they could not assess the value of what they were being sold as a world view.[51]

Grayling's proposed strategy for 'countering the pernicious effects that faith and dogma can produce' is, among other things, to 'find major ways of reversing the current trend of falling enrolment in science courses':

> The alternative is a return to the Dark Ages, the tips of whose shadows are coldly falling upon us even now.[52]

Must we all become scientists or shut up? Harding asked some time ago now, 'Whose Science?':

> We must 'invent' the very Western sciences and institutions of knowledge in which we participate (and which pay some of our salaries) as bizarre beliefs and practices of the indigenous peoples who rule the modern West. We must master their techniques as we simultaneously continue to 'discover' the ways in which they are 'other' to ourselves and our agendas.[53]

For Bataille, 'the truth that science reveals is stripped of human sense' since the phenomenon of science is only one of a number of symptoms of the loss of the 'virile unity' of '*life*':

> The life thus broken into three pieces has ceased to be *life*; it is nothing more than art, science, or politics ... The renunciation of life in exchange for function is the condition consented to by each of them. A few scientists have artistic or political concerns, and politicians and artists can also look outside their fields; they only add up three infirmities, which together do not make a valid man. A totality of life has little to do with a collection of abilities and areas of expertise. One can no more cut it into pieces than one can cut up a living body. Life is the virile unity of the pieces that go to make it up. In it there is the simplicity of an axe blow.[54]

Critical 'transgression' has long since limited itself to speaking of the arcane forces of 'sexuality' as a fundamentally liberating social or psychic disturbance. We remain preoccupied with the kaleidoscopic relationships creating libidinal intensities between human bodies, rather than between human consciousness and its reality. Even for Foucault, sexuality was central to transgression *because* it indicated the loss of a sacred context for contemporary profanities:

We like to believe that sexuality has regained, in contemporary experience, its full truth as a process of nature, a truth which has long been lingering in the shadows and hiding under various disguises – until now, that is, when our positive awareness allows us to decipher it so that it may at last emerge in the clear light of language. Yet, never did sexuality enjoy a more immediately natural understanding and never did it know a greater 'felicity of expression' than in the Christian world of fallen bodies and of sin. The proof is its whole tradition of mysticism and spirituality which was incapable of dividing the continuous forms of desire, of rapture, of penetration, of ecstasy, of that outpouring which leaves us spent: all of these experiences seemed to lead, without interruption or limit, right to the heart of a divine love of which they were both the outpouring and the source returning upon itself. What characterizes modern sexuality from Sade to Freud is not its having found the language of its logic or of its natural process, but rather, through the violence done by such languages, its having been 'denatured' – cast into an empty zone where it achieves whatever meagre form is bestowed upon it by the establishment of its limits. Sexuality points to nothing beyond itself, no prolongation, except in a frenzy which disrupts it. We have not in the least liberated sexuality, though we have, to be exact, carried it to its limits.[55]

It is precisely in an unflinching, loving embrace of the defiled elements of privileged knowledge that Bataillean consciousness experiences totality. Totality is the ever-elusive experience screened by the object of desire: 'The Object of Desire is the Universe, or the Totality of Being'. This 'most familiar thing' is also 'the hardest to comprehend' because it is 'truly alien to ordinary reflection in that it includes at the same time objective reality and the subject who perceives the objective reality':

We can keep this much in mind: that in the embrace the object of desire is always the totality of being, just as it is the object of religion or art, . . . the object of desire is the *universe*, in the form of she who in the embrace is the mirror, where we ourselves are reflected.[56]

Bataille's preoccupation with embracing the debased and feminine 'object of desire' was not only theoretical. He was an empiricist of the highest order and famously spent a fortune in the brothels of Paris. One can only wonder at the experience of a Parisian prostitute (especially his favourite, Violet, who transferred brothels to avoid his excessive attentions) finding herself faced with this quiet-spoken, unusually intellectual, peculiarly conscious and conscientious client. Did she know he thought her 'GOD' or 'the *universe*' and that he was encountering totality when he came to her? More to the point perhaps, is it really possible to take seriously a *liberatory* critical movement founded in the very limited mode of transgression available to an economically free man snatching furtive moments of continuity from an economically objectified woman?

This would be less interesting, perhaps, if Bataille had not long-since become 'fundamental' to a 'whole generation' of influential critical theorists, including Jean Baudrillard, Jean-François Lyotard and Giles Deleuze:

> In addition to Foucault, Barthes and Sollers, Jacques Derrida, Julia Kristeva, Jean-Joseph Goux and, supremely, Denis Hollier, among other contributors to [*Tel Quel*], elaborated their own theoretical reflections by way of Bataille's texts.[57]

Bataille is a highly infectious source for contemporary critical theory. In his own terms, the source of this particular intellectual virus lay in an erotic embrace with the body and mind of a woman:

> The world of lovers is no less *true* than that of politics. It even absorbs the totality of life, which politics cannot do. And its characteristics are not those of the fragmentary and empty world of practical action, but those that belong to *human life* before it is reduced to servility: the world of lovers is constructed, like life, out of a *series of chances that give the awaited answer to an avid and powerful will to be.*[58]

Bataille made it quite clear that he did not have his most important ideas alone, but alongside or in exchange with, his female lover; Colette Peignot (Laure): 'Laure and I often thought the barrier separating us was crumbling'. He writes passionately of one particular experience of 'communion' that occurred as Colette was dying:

> During the last days of Laure's illness, the afternoon of November 2, I had come to the passage [in writing *The Sacred*] where I express the similarity between our quest for the 'grail' and the objects of religion. I ended it with this sentence: 'Christianity has *substantialized* the sacred, but the nature of the sacred, in which we recognize today the burning existence of religion, is perhaps what is most elusive among men, the sacred being only a privileged moment of communal unity, a moment of convulsive communication of what ordinarily is stifled.' I immediately added in the margin to indicate clearly, at least to myself, the meaning of the last lines: 'identical to love.'

Bataille then recorded noticing that Colette/Laure had 'a small, white, paper folder that bore the title "The Sacred"'. On reading the papers in this folder after her death, he says:

> Reading all her writings, which were entirely unknown to me, provoked without a doubt one of the most violent emotions of my life, but nothing struck me and wrenched me more than the last sentence of the texts in which she speaks of the Sacred. I had never been able to express to her the paradoxical idea that the sacred is *communication*. I had only arrived at this idea the very moment I expressed it, a few minutes before noticing that Laure had entered the throes of death. I can say with utter precision that nothing I had ever expressed to her could even have approached this idea.[59]

Bataille initiated for the European critical tradition a powerful figure of transgression that finds orgasm, salvation and death isomorphic. This figure is now deeply involved in our critical encounters with each other, with writing and with the world. Bataille is certainly acknowledged as the Name-of-the-Father of Transgression. Less acknowledged is his most transgressive idea: that his thoughts were not his alone. Bataille caught transgression from his very close encounters with women.

A dedicated Catholic in his mid-twenties, Bataille had chosen to live a 'saintly' life. This powerful will to spiritual purity permeates his first (and often neglected) published work, *Notre-Dame de Rhiems* (1918). In this pious account of the architecture, history and religious significance of Rhiems cathedral, Bataille identified the cathedral itself with 'the highest and most marvellous consolation left with us by God . . . a mother for whom we die'.[60] Between 1922 and 1924 he underwent a second, reverse conversion: 'At the start of 1922, Bataille was still devout or at least humble before God. By the end of 1924 he was leading "the most dissolute lifestyle".[61] Bataille's biographer leads us through a chain of reading that led to Bataille's abandonment of his early, passionate Christianity: Sade, Proust, Gide, Dostoevsky and, of course, Nietzsche. Bataille credited his own inverse conversion to a transformative experience of sexualized women: 'My true church is a whorehouse – the only one that gives me true satisfaction'.[62] He writes of himself at this time in the third person:

> Two months in England in 1920. Following a stay with the Benedictines of Quarr Abbey on the Isle of Wight, suddenly loses his faith because his Catholicism has caused a woman he loved to shed tears.[63]

The idea of radical 'continuity' that coheres the complexities and contradictions of Bataille's prolific thought was something he could not have thought alone, something that should always also be credited to the advanced wisdom of the voiceless women who taught him transgression: 'divine was the message of shame I learned from a prostitute's body'.[64] It should also be at least partly credited to the largely unacknowledged work (erotic and literary) of Colette Peignot (Laure). Bataille's intellectual transgression emerged from a closer than usual engagement with the arcane strangeness of embodied femininity.

The embrace of the 'object of desire' – woman or GOD – always approaches totality of being:

> She is vast, she is distant like the darkness in which she has trouble breathing, and she is so truly the vastness of the universe in her cries, her silences are so truly the emptiness of death, which is the absence of bounds to the universe. But between her and me there is a kind of appeasement which, denoting rebellion and apathy at the same time, eliminates the distance that separated us from each other, and the one that separated us both from the universe.[65]

But is this experience of the 'Totality of the Real' explored by Bataille, of being at least momentarily one with the universe, only available to (heterosexual) men embracing women?

> Two beings of the opposite sex are lost in one another and together form a new being different from either. The precariousness of this new being is obvious: it is never something whose parts are distinct from it; there is no more than a tendency to lose consciousness in brief moments of darkness.[66]

Two sexuate beings, then, lost in one another, together form a new being that exists momentarily beyond the constraints of the profane world. An experience of continuity, of 'fusion', between the lovers is an experience of the 'absence of bounds to the universe'. When the experiential distance between the lovers is eliminated, both can find a momentary encounter with totality, and it seems common sense to assume that totality would involve a common consciousness that was not limited by the bounded perspective of 'difference'. As Sheri I. Hoem has shown, the object of Bataille's analysis is otherness in the form of the 'feminine' herself:

> The 'phantasmatic tendency' of naming the feminine continues to invade even non-traditional, postmodern thinking ... the feminine is objectified as not only an absolutely feminine but the absolutely other on the order of a thing.[67]

The transformation of difference is always at work in the sexual embrace, but strangely heightened in the specifically 'heterosexual' experience of sexual and reproductive 'fusion'. That most basic and debased human encounter touches upon an otherwise unimaginable potential for boundless continuity with existence: orgasm prefigures a greater, final release from bounded individual embodied life. Death feels like coming, then.

> The negation of nature (of animality) is what separates us from the concrete totality: it inserts us in the abstractions of a human order – where, like so many artful fairies, work, science and bureaucracy change us into abstract entities. But the embrace restores us, not to nature (which is itself, if it is not reintegrated, only a detached part), but rather to the totality in which man has his share by *losing himself*. For an embrace is not just a fall into the animal muck, but the anticipation of death, and of the putrefaction that follows it.[68]

Through an erotic encounter Bataille figures the sacred experience of totality; suspension of the otherwise profane experience of non-continuity (dualism). This might be considered a radically conservative dream. On this note it is worth heeding Bataille's self-proclaimed and counter-intuitive sexual conservatism, as noted by Slavoj Žižek:

> Bataille was fully aware of how this transgressive 'passion for the Real' *relies on prohibition*; this is why he was explicitly opposed to the 'sexual revolution,' to the rise of sexual permissiveness which began in his last years: 'I must first make plain the futility of the common contention that sexual taboos are nothing but prejudice, and it is high time we were rid of them ... I am opposed to the tendency which seems today to be sweeping [them] away. I am not among those who see the neglect of sexual interdictions as a solution. I even think that human potential depends on these interdictions'.[69]

Bataille continues:

> The shame, the modesty sensed in connection with the strong sense of pleasure, would be, so the argument [for sexual liberation] runs, mere proofs of backwardness and unintelligence. Which is the equivalent of saying that we ought to undertake a thorough housecleaning, set fire to our house and take to the woods, returning to the good old days of animalism, of devouring whoever we please.[70]

Surya's reference to Bataille's apparently contradictory claim to sexual conservatism draws attention to the synergy between Bataille and Lacan on matters of sexual interdiction and sexual difference:

> Can one imagine Georges Bataille and Jacques Lacan to be profoundly in agreement on this point? It is not inconceivable that this would have been a major subject of conversation between them. It should not be

forgotten in fact that they regularly met in Guitrancourt, at Lacan's home, among other places.[71]

It's not inconceivable that they shared some ideas about sexual interdiction when they had, after all, shared a wife. Sylvia Maklès, Bataille's first wife, went on to marry Lacan. She was an actress. She kept Bataille's name for herself and his daughter Laurence, and also – for legal reasons – passed it to Lacan's own daughter, Judith. Bataille had known Lacan probably since 1933 and Lacan seems to have had a hand in the development of the pre-war Acéphalic activities. Bataille met his second wife, Diane Kotchoubey, when she visited a house he had rented close by for Lacan and Sylvia in the village of Vezelay, where he took shelter from the war in the summer of 1943. The best discussion of Bataille's direct but unacknowledged impact on Lacanian psychoanalysis I have found is in Fred Botting and Scott Wilson's *Bataille*, which contains this suggestive anecdote:

> On one occasion [Bataille] and Lacan were going to Sylvia's apartment to lunch, and as they went upstairs Lacan said proudly, 'We're going to see my wife. As you know she's Sylvia *Bataille*'.[72]

The transgression set in train by Bataille, or at least brought into play by him from a heady mix of de Sade's extreme materialist enlightenment and Nietszche's sovereign dissolution, is not in itself a plea for the overcoming of prohibitions so much as a heightened consciousness of the imperative structures and processes which allow the experience of transgression to be possible in the first place: 'human potential depends on these interdictions'. Bataille was not an advocate of 'sexual liberation'. One of the key sites for his model of transgression is marriage: 'I take marriage to be a transgression then'.[73] This is only common sense: transgression is made *possible* through its negation of a web of relatively stable, collectively experienced sexual interdictions (taboo). However, this leaves us with what Slavoj Žižek has called Bataille's 'premodern' dilemma:

> He remains stuck in this dialectic of the Law and its transgression, of the prohibitive Law as generating the transgressive desire, which forces him to the debilitating perverse conclusion that one has to install prohibitions in order to be able to enjoy their violation – a clearly unworkable pragmatic paradox.[74]

In terms of the geological figure with which I began, transgression can only be experienced when there is a recognized border between the land and the sea. Sexual interdiction is not so much a 'prejudice' to be overcome, then, as a boundary implicit in simply being human. The contemporary critical work that claims the name of transgression takes as its aim the final liberation of uninhibited sexual activity, by experimental practice that breaches traditional categories and promises to give free reign to the preconscious forces previously harnessed by conventional heterosexuality. And there is something to be said for this indeed. The problem is, of course, that successive waves of 'sexual liberation' finally erode conditions for the experience of the sacred in transgression central to Bataille's thought experiments. Or maybe that isn't a problem, just the point. We are not really prepared to accept the transgressive thought of the possibility of such a common sacrament, and instead turn sexual cartwheels in the sand.[75] The alternative is an unthinkable return to sexual morality. Or is it? Each generation finds its own mode of transgression in its struggle for sexual liberation and freedom. Give them something to transgress, then, or they may finally look to overturn elemental prohibitions; those which even the most 'liberated' would still want repressed.

For Roland Barthes, Bataille's narrative of the *Eye* is not even really pornographic. The narrative under a Barthesian analysis performs a 'transgression of values that is the avowed principle of eroticism'. This transgression reiterates a 'technical transgression of the forms of language' through a serious 'play of metaphor and metonymy'. What '*Story of the Eye* makes it possible ultimately to transgress is sex'.[76] *Story of the Eye* is not pornography in the common sense of represented sexual fantasy. If it *were* simply a sexual fantasy, notes Barthes, 'the first thing requiring explanation would be why the erotic theme is never directly phallic (what we have here is a "round phallicism")'.[77] The *Eye* as a narrative transgresses 'sex', then, at the intersection of language, affect and material body. The first chain of metaphorical organization Barthes finds in the *Eye* is 'varied through a number of substitute objects ... all globular ... called something different': egg, roundness, saucer of milk, dead eye in its socket, castrated testicle. The second chain presents 'all the avatars of liquid, an image linked equally with eye, egg, and balls'.[78] When the chains cross, you have an eye weeping. You might also glimpse the baby's eye-view of a globular breast lactating.

Bataille put into circulation a denial of his mother's place in the *Story of the Eye*: '[i]t is impossible for me to say positively that Marcelle is basically identical with my mother'.[79] Marcelle is the girl who dies in *Story of the Eye*; the third term in the narrator's 'relationship' with

Simone, over whose dead body they finally consummate their passion. Marie-Antoinette, Bataille's mother, was married to a syphilitic husband who provided her with two sons nonetheless, the second (Georges Bataille) born following his father's blindness and not long before his paralysis. Bataille's mother abandoned her husband to take her sons out of the devastation of Rheims. His father died blind, alone and insane a year later. Bataille gives us in 'Coincidences' his remembered father's extraordinary image as the key to *Story of the Eye*, published under a pseudonym in 1928; the year in which he married Sylvia Maklès and left his mother at the age of 31.

> When I was born, my father was suffering from general paralysis, and he was already blind when he conceived me; not long after my birth, his sinister disease confined him to an armchair. However, the very contrary of most male babies, who are in love with their mothers, I was in love with my father.[80]

The rolling eyes of the syphilitic father have merged with the weeping breasts of the suffering mother, who had sustained the life of her boys in spite of her own (quite reasonable) foray into madness following her husband's death: 'Since he could not see anything, his pupils very frequently pointed up into space, shifting under the lids, and this happened particularly when he pissed'.

Bataille was uncompromising in his representational treatment of mothers: Simone's mother is pissed on by her daughter; Bataille's late work, *My Mother*, makes the narrator's mother the agent of his seduction into a life of degenerate dissolution, culminating in incest and death; the narrator of *Blue of Noon* masturbates before his mother's corpse.[81] The mother is always present in, or more accurately *as*, the scene of transgression: the literary son transgresses in narrative to avoid a greater evil.

Julia Kristeva is explicit about the maternal metaphor at work in Bataille's 'borderline writing' which 'in other civilizations and times had analogies in the mystical tradition':

> All these tendencies, to which could be added postfuturist or postsurrealist writings, demonstrate a basic realignment in style that can be interpreted as an exploration of the typical imaginary relationship, that to the mother, through the most radical and problematic aspect of this relationship, language.[82]

Given that GOD for Bataillean thought is a prostitute, the idea of the non-existence of God that underpins his thought experiments is equivalent to Lacan's non-existence of the (sexual) woman. By thinking God out of existence, but holding on to the sacred as a possibility, Bataille elevates the feminine (but what a feminine!) to the place of GOD: in accordance with the banal, material reality that the body of a woman is always the worldly creator of 'man': 'A horrifyingly simple testimony to God's existence'.[83]

Bataille's ungraspable concept of GOD finds an awesome metonym in Madame Edwarda's gaping 'vulva':

> The narrator of *Madame Edwarda* proceeds to kiss the whore's 'rags' as the Christian mystics kiss the wounds of Christ. There can be little doubt that Bataille imagines the vulva as a wound, but this is not because of a negative relation to castration. Far from being an excised penis, the vulva is a complex terrain of contact with death, of exactly the kind castration proscribes.[84]

I will limit myself here to saying that I am reminded of that joke by Houellebecq's sick 'comedian':

> 'Do you know what they call the fat stuff around the vagina?'
> 'No.'
> 'The woman'.[85]

This chain of literal association does not pass without its problems, and for the woman (rather than only her 'vulva') to be 'GOD' she must also be defiled. Defiled mothers are central to the narrative adventures of theoretical erotics.[86] No wonder, when the desired 'suspension of non-continuity' is apprehended directly in sub-sequent, psychoanalytically inflected writings, as a 'pre-Oedipal', 'semiotic' or 'intra-uterine' continuity of one with another. Subjectivity is theoretically founded in the fundamental human experience of infantile bodily and psychic separation from 'the mother' that determines an individual subject's relationship to language and therefore reality. Thus much is familiar, explored at length and from different angles by Freud, Lacan, Kristeva and Irigaray among others. It has also been recognized at work in a particularly 'masculine' form in Bataille:

> What does appear to me certain is that there will be no genuine renewal ... as long as every drama, whether textual or sexual, continues to be envisaged – as in Bataille's pornography and in Harold Bloom's theory of poetry – in terms of a confrontation between an all-powerful father and a traumatized son, a confrontation staged across and over the body of the mother.[87]

Denis Hollier in turn understands transgressive eroticism as a simple 'absence of repression':

> Whereas in neurosis most sexual drives, particularly those condemned by moral and social authorities, are only manifested under the disguise of symptomatic transpositions, the absence of repression allows them to appear, untransposed, in the life of those who are perverse. In this sense, the absence of repression makes perversion a sort of return to or sustaining of infant sexuality.[88]

He associates the maternal metaphor underlying Bataille's transgression with the cathedral that dominates his first encounter with writing:

> All of Bataille's writing would be aimed at the destruction of this cathedral; to reduce it to silence he would write against this text. Not, in a fetishistic fixation with some sort of original sin, against this text alone, against these six pages that in retrospect are so incongruous, but against the veiled ideological necessity controlling it, against a far vaster and more secret cathedral in which it is thoroughly trapped and which somehow prevents it having been written, which makes writing only possible *afterward* and against this text, against the oppressive architecture of constructive values.[89]

Are 'constructive values' always 'oppressive'? Is architecture really such an evil? Human life would be a lot less comfortable, and certainly less sustainable, without it. The Christian architecture of the cathedral that Bataille explodes in his later work is for Hollier 'dominated by every feminine and maternal value'. Maternal authority is that 'far vaster and more secret cathedral in which it is thoroughly trapped' and *'against'* which Bataille finds himself forced to transgress. Is his transgression just the excitable anxiety of the son on breaching maternal authority in his (sexualized) turn to others? All boys have to reject the 'veiled ideological necessity' of maternal authority to develop their unique identity. There is really no need to make such a fuss about it.

Bataille is most famous for his genuinely appalling tales of sexual excess, but it is worth pausing to remind ourselves that he is at the same time thoroughly preoccupied with the transformative experience of 'love':

> [love is] the full and limitless being unconfined within the trammels of separate personalities, continuity of being, glimpsed as a deliverance through the person of the beloved. There is something absurd and

horribly commixed about this conception, yet beyond the absurdity, the confusion and the suffering there lies a miraculous truth.[90]

Bataille had loved Colette/Laure. He also 'loved' the prostitutes of Paris. His encounters with these women provides a structural form for his thinking on eroticism more generally. The embrace that centres his figure for transgression is always incommensurate for a start: *his* desire can never really coincide with *hers*, given that the prostitute's eroticism is economically, rather than spiritually, determined and experienced. She who 'allows him to come' does so for survival; but a mode of survival that denies her the normal decencies associated with being human. He who understood that the shameful is sanctified did not 'think it necessary to examine each of the situations [he had] spoken of from a woman's point of view'.

I had to pause there to avoid the temptation to slip into sarcasm: peace to his *manes*. Following the insane logic of Bataille, the point is that those 'normal decencies associated with being human' are finally worthless compared to the unthinkable divinity enraptured in the reviled matter of the universe. In the post-Enlightenment rational profanity of industrialized social life, the negation of nature that forges the human-animal seems to be at its peak, and the object of that negation returns to haunt the human dream of transcendent reason. It returns in a form associated with the sacred, and testifies to a reality beyond the concerns of production and reproduction. More to the point, it returns *female*: gaping, material, viscous, emotional, irrational, obscene. This realization might indeed be expected to have induced abject horror in the male theorist, fully represented in his narrator's anguished sight of Edwarda's divine 'rag and ruin'. The experience of this thought is unmistakably different for a girl.

What does the little girl recoil from, whatever her age? *From Madame Edwarda.*[91]

Lyotard, in his own extraordinary account of 'the innocent Little Girl Marx', identifies in Edwarda the archetype for 'the system of capital' in itself:

> Edwarda's exposed vulva, her fainting fit in the street . . . , her return in a taxi, copulating with some driver culminating in a gushing, bruising orgasm – this is what capital promises male and female lovers of organic bodies and affective harmonies. Capital is not the denaturation of relations between man and man, nor between man and woman, it is the wavering of the (imaginary?) primacy of genitality, of reproduction and sexual difference, it is the displacement of what was in place, it is the unbinding of the most insane pulsions, since money is the sole justification or bond, and money being able to justify anything, it deresponsibilizes and *raves* absolutely . . .[92]

Lyotard's raving sentence goes on for another five clauses. But I only meant to say that Lyotard, in the midst of his unbounded sentences, produces the glimmer of an intelligent account of the otherwise inexplicable Edwarda:

> prostitution is the model of the relationship in capitalist society . . . in the immense and vicious circuit of capitalist exchanges, whether of commodities or 'services', it appears that *all the modalities of jouissance* are possible and that none is ostracized.[93]

Edwarda's iconic 'madness' is the activity of a prostitute enjoying and giving freely:

> The taxi driver will have shot his load as if it has been just another lay; but he will have paid nothing, and finally it is insanity itself he held and penetrated, and not neutral venal flesh. Edwarda the prostitute journeys beyond every pimp's organization, but in the same place, on the same terrain as this organization . . . One equality is order; and the other, which is the same, but without the pimp and money, is the subversion of this order.[94]

Edwarda circulates in Bataille's mysterious little narrative as the arch-transgressive figure of the prostitute abandoning herself to a manic desire without claiming payment. The narrator watches, and narrates, while she takes her simple pleasure from the (I am tempted to say unfortunate) taxi driver. Lyotard's analysis of Edwarda has become central to transgressive critical politics. She now stands in for CAPITALISM as well as GOD:

> Starting from the Marxian premise that the standard capitalist social relation is one of prostitution, Lyotard's point in using the figure of

Edwarda, the mad and enjoying prostitute, is twofold: first to refute the 'denial prior to analysis, the idea that capitalism deprives us of intensities as affects', and second, to suggest that while the 'bar' that separates staff from client produces the fiction necessary for *jouissance*, Madame Edwarda, in her 'madness', 'is in the process of transforming' her place of work into 'a place where intensities emerge within political economy'.[95]

But what does Edwarda, the 'mad and enjoying' prostitute, experience? The 'woman's point of view' is as unimaginable as GOD's in this narrative. This does not necessarily mean that it is a view occluded, or that Bataille did not recognize there must *be* another point of view, since his desire for 'Totality' is expressed through a synthesis of the sexual dialectic.

Bataille's narrative heroines act out a rabid mode of obscene, self-pleasuring femininity for his narration. It would be too easy to criticize his preoccupation with the mad and debased prostitute and the corrosive effect of this figure on his critical thought. At this point I would rather draw your attention to the unusual extent to which women are *overwhelmingly present* in Bataille's thought. He never seems to think (theorize or narrate) without involving women. 'Involving' is not a strong enough term here: except perhaps in the sense of 'being involved' with someone. Bataille's women (internal and external to his writing) are unremittingly sexual. Their sexuality is the material from which his theoretical and narrative work is formed. One need only consider Edwarda's gaping vulva to be struck by the degree to which the irrepressible materiality of female-embodiment is the key to Bataille's critical transgression. This overwhelming presence is perhaps most *acutely* emphasized when we compare him with his intellectual apprentices: Lacan and Foucault. I'll focus on Foucault in the next chapter, but suffice to say Lacan effectively dematerialized his theoretical feminine to the point of no return, after which we might *all* 'become woman': 'putting on the stereotypes of femininity'.[96] Inheriting Bataille's woman (or his ideas for that matter) probably does something to a man in the end.

Bataille's relationship with Colette Peignot (Laure) remains to be explored. She more than matched his desire for excess, and yet she also complained in characteristically womanly terms at his mode of loving:

Scatter, spoil, destroy, throw to the dogs all that you want: you will never affect me again. I will never be where you think you find me, where you think you've finally caught me in a chokehold that makes you come ... *Everything* you have been doing, I've known about – *everything* ...[97]

Not that she was sitting at home washing the dishes and tending the babies. Born 1903 in Paris, she died at the age of 35 in Bataille's home, experiencing along the way a life of desperate and mostly miserable intensity about which she wrote fully and frankly. Her first affair ended in a failed suicide attempt. In Berlin from 1928, she lived with a sadist who would make her wear dog collars and walk on all fours, and who regularly beat her. A talented student of Russian, she travelled to the Soviet Union in 1930 to live with the peasants. Bataille picks up the story:

> She lived there first in poverty and solitude, eating in miserable restaurants and only rarely setting foot in the opulent hotels for foreigners . . . Weary of everything, she wanted to get to know and even share the life of the Russian peasants. In the middle of winter, she insisted on being taken to a family of poor mujiks in an isolated village. She withstood this excessively harsh trial poorly. She was hospitalized in Moscow, gravely ill. Her brother came to fetch her and brought her back in a sleeping car.[98]

One wonders what the peasants made of her attention? Did they feed her, give her precious space, to allow her to explore and understand the true experience of poverty? I am minded of Simone Weil (critical friend of Bataille, and probable figure behind the character of Lazare in *Blue of Noon* according to Surya):

> Formerly, in adult education centres for the people, workers used sometimes to say, with a sort of timid eagerness, to intellectuals calling themselves Marxists: 'We should very much like to know what dialectical materialism is'. There is little likelihood that they were ever satisfied.[99]

Colette Peignot's writings were unpublished until her death and Bataille's discovery of 'The Sacred' among her papers. They are compelling to read.

> What if Nietzsche did more for the liberation of man than Lenin? The rich man or poor man constructs his own greatness in his heart, his faculty to resist what exists, to compromise life as it is intended: soiled and ruined by millions of people. To exist *against* and not *with*.[100]

Bataille famously posited the defiled, desiring feminine as GOD. Laure, in precise dialectical response, wrote of 'The God – Bataille'.[101]

It must have been an interesting relationship. Milo Sweedler has noted that Colette Peignot's writing, edited and illegally published by

Bataille under the pseudonym of 'Laure' in 1939, was distributed only to the 'unavowed community' that circled the pair:

> In the months following her death – from tuberculosis at the age of thirty-five – Bataille published a selection of her writings under the title *Le Sacré*. The publication of this book violated the wishes of the Peignot family, who had the legal rights to the papers in question ... Without any indication from the publishing house (Deux Artisans, apparently), the run was limited to 200 numbered copies, personally given by the editor to a select group of readers, whose names are inscribed in the respective copies. But there may be other, more theoretically based reasons for restricting this community of readers. Laure's writings are *déchirants* (heartrending, harrowing, agonizing, wounding, lacerating) ... They risk performing on the reader the violence that they describe.[102]

According to Sweedler, '[l]overs "communicate" through their wounds'. Communication is also available to the writer, but 'only if the wound that he or she exposes finds a corresponding opening on the part of the reader'.[103] The wounds that allow for communication also make sexual fusion possible:

> Bodies open out to a state of continuity through secret channels that give us a feeling of obscenity.[104]

Similar 'wounds' are also argued by Bataille to be manifest in mystical experience, or 'religious eroticism', which 'is concerned with the fusion of beings with a world beyond everyday reality'. But '[o]nly the beloved can in this world bring about what our human limitations deny, a total blending of two beings, a continuity between two discontinuous creatures'.[105] We follow transgression only to be brought back to love.

Colette/Laure is, then, 'at once marginal and central' to Bataille's work:

> Laure remains among the most provocative and elusive figures of the twentieth-century French avant-garde ... What we retain of her contribution to cultural history is largely via her role in Bataille's communitarian projects, where she functions as a martyr to the community. The religious connotations are hard to overlook ... Laure becomes the figurehead of an unavowable community, as Blanchot's locution would have it.[106]

So there is Bataille, lost in Laure till her death in 1938, which crystallized a new mode of his thought into consciousness ('*death* has taken the name of Laure'), seething in the background of contemporary critical thought, reaching the surface in little bubbles of well-punctuated arguments for literary and critical transgression.[107] Or, more fittingly, in Chris Jenks' (probably unconscious) image:

> The literature by, on or about Bataille has proliferated and he is now seen, increasingly, to be a central and seminal figure – a fame that he would have resented for mainstreaming his maverick thoughts.[108]

Pefanis has described Bataille's presence in contemporary critical thought as 'like the movement of a large, dark body, maybe a black hole, whose presence in the heavens has been discernible in the erratic orbits of the visible planets'.[109] It is the nature of black holes to absorb everything in their vicinity. Transgression has a tendency to proliferate. It is catching. More problematic than this, since most of us recover our senses in the end, in forwarding its proliferation some recent critics have taken transgression to levels of influence to which it can only really have a metaphoric claim:

> This is the new dawn of epistemology and ontology, there is an existentialism here, a seismic sociological message and the seeds of the postmodern. In many senses transgression of the foundations of Western social life has become a necessity.

Jenks goes on to argue (with some considerable confidence) that:

> If God is indeed dead then all that proceeds in the name of religion is a lie, an absurdity or at best a distortion.

If God is in the grammar, Jenks' use of the exclamation mark may indeed testify to his 'absence':

> Transgression and its capacity to challenge, fracture, overthrow, spoil or question the unquestionable can no longer be contained as naughtiness or occasional abhorration. Transgression is part of the purpose of being and is the unstable principle by which any stasis either sustains or transforms. This does not make all transgressions either 'good' or 'bad', it renders them purposive. In the same way, all rules are neither 'good' nor 'bad' and their sanctity no longer resides in the judgement of God![110]

With God 'dead', there is 'no limit to infinity' and so 'we are forced' to recognize 'our' sovereignty: 'the monocausality of the self'. There are 'wonderful possibilities bestowed on humankind and on human thought through the death of God':

> Transgression has become a modern, post-God initiative, a searching for limits to break, an eroticism that goes beyond the limits of sexuality.[111]

How tiring continuously to *search for* limits to break: what would happen if we learned to accept our limitations and live within them? I am concerned by a strong tendency emerging in critical work to glorify and glamorize images and examples of transgression:

> In practice, of course, all contemporary transgressions relate to the mad, bad and dangerous because pre-post-structuralist life, that is, everyday life, is riven with code, binary, law, opposition and negation, and indeed anything but genealogy as its method. The Moors murderers, the Kray Twins, the James Bulger killers, Osama bin Laden cannot be seen as either outside of or ahead of their time, they are oppositional manifestations, they are significations of evil and darkness, we claim their limits as our consensus and we actually fight for the right of such recognition (in a way that Hegel would have understood).[112]

Transgression is the inverted limit of human potential, the point of reversal. We now seem increasingly to face a moral obligation to transgress in the name of liberation:

> What we cannot escape, as if it were some straightforward academic decision, is the emotional turbulence and categorical disruption that Bataille's thoughts provoke.[113]

This is all very well and good, but 'emotional turbulence' and 'categorical disruption' are no longer enough for me. In any case, I can get plenty of 'emotional disturbance' and 'categorical disruption' for free by sitting down for a meal with my family. Emotional turbulence is a very common experience for most people, perhaps less so for academic readers and writers who have the professional leisure to spend too much time reading and thinking about Bataille. What we now need is a model of transgression that does not rest with 'emotional turbulence' or transitory states of bodily ecstasy. These extreme states of 'limit' consciousness seem to demand the defilement and even death of the object. I desire a transgression that passes these as transitional on the way to a more lasting and *universal* model of liberation. Transgression without anguish would be another way to put it.

2

Minerva's Owl:
the quest for feminine agency and
the freedom of necessity

It is decisively important in this movement that the search, intellectually undertaken at the promptings of unsatisfied desire, has always preceded theory's delineation of the object sought. The belated intervention of discriminating intelligence certainly opened up a field of possibilities for empty error, whose extent became discouraging, but it is no less certain that an experience of this nature would not have been possible if some clairvoyant theory had tried to fix in advance its direction and its limits. It is only when things are already settled and night has fallen that the 'Owl of Minerva' can give the goddess an account of the events that have taken place and decide upon their hidden meaning.[114] (Bataille)

My father leaps up
in the high space
and the mother I thought was lost
ricochets
round him. Strong
arches and vaults of flesh
enclose them. These
two make the sculptured air.
They are the architects. This
design is their dance.[115] (Michèle Roberts)

She lets the other come.[116] (Hoem)

Even on such a cursory examination of Bataille's erotic intellectual work, it could be asserted that the field of criticism and theory has inherited a diminished rendering of transgression in the generational transition from Bataille to Foucault. There is a formal inadequacy between Bataille's transgressive plenitude and the more recent emergence of a moral obligation to transgress: virtuous transgression. One aspect lost in that inadequacy concerns the central place of the female-embodied mind and experience in Bataille's thought of transgression. Foucault worked to inaugurate transgression in critical thought:

> Perhaps one day [transgression] will seem as decisive for our culture, as much a part of its soil, as the experience of contradiction was at an earlier time for dialectical thought. But in spite of so many scattered signs, the language in which transgression will find its space and the illumination of its being lies almost entirely in the future.[117]

That future is now here. Botting and Scott call this Foucault's prophetic claim and note its subsequent fulfilment:

> almost instantly fulfilling Foucault's prophecy, a 'discourse on transgression' – which is to say, an academic discourse in which the signifier 'transgression' is a key word – has established itself in Britain and America in the twenty or so years since Foucault's essay was translated into English. This discourse, associated with cultural studies and literary theory, a discourse with a wide range of interests from Medieval and Renaissance carnival to shifting sexual practices in modernity, has in many ways taken over from a Hegelian-Marxist critique concerned with contradiction as the important focus for radical academic circles.[118]

They also note, however, that the discourse of transgression initiated by Foucault's account of Bataille 'repeats many of the gestures and assumptions it imagined it had superseded'. One of those gestures is the elision of the central and productive place of female-embodied thought.

I have already suggested that Bataille's transgression consciously incorporated and evaded the 'woman's point of view' as content because he was in a passionate dialectical encounter with the 'hope and terror' of femininity:

> And just as virility is tied to the allure of a nude body, full existence is tied to any image that arouses hope and terror. THE LOVED ONE in this broken-up world has become the only power that has retained the virtue returning to the heat of life.[119]

His privileged moment of the subject in dissolution (the brief non-continuous experience of continuity) has been well-argued by Carolyn Dean and Judith Starkis to assume a ' "masculine" subject who initially possesses a position of self to transgress or lose'. Yes, but this avowedly 'masculine' subject articulates the need for intimacy with female-embodied thought in order to experience its own transgression:

> The whole business of eroticism is to strike to the inmost core of the living being, so that the heart stands still. The transition from the normal state to that of erotic desire presupposes a partial dissolution of the person as he exists in the realm of discontinuity. Dissolution – this expression corresponds with *dissolute life*, the familiar phrase linked with

erotic activity. In the process of dissolution, the male partner has generally an active role, while the female partner is passive. The passive, female role is essentially the one that is dissolved as a separate entity. But for the male partner the dissolution of the passive partner means only one thing: it is paving the way for a fusion where both are mingled, attaining at length the same degree of dissolution. The whole business of eroticism is to destroy the self-contained character of the participants as they are in their normal lives.[120]

The passive partner in the erotic exchange, normatively gendered female, provides the conditions for the 'fusion' that releases an experience of continuity. Women are, as Judith Starkis has noted, 'prominent in Bataille's theory of erotic transgression; they are instrumental to the enactment of *masculine* self-loss'.[121] This is at least in part because the presence of female-embodiment is, for Bataille, the primary *condition* for an experience of 'fusion'.

'Fusion' is central to Bataille's account of *Eroticism*, at least as much so as the more fashionable concept of 'transgression'. Erotic transgression at its height is an overtly religious experience of 'fusion':

If we observe the taboo, if we submit to it, we are no longer conscious of it. But in the act of violating it we feel the anguish of mind without which the taboo could not exist: that is the experience of sin. That experience leads to the completed transgression, the successful transgression which, in maintaining the prohibition, maintains it in order to benefit by it. The inner experience of eroticism demands from the subject a sensitiveness to the anguish at the heart of the taboo no less great than the desire which leads him to infringe it. This is religious sensibility, and it always links desire closely with terror, intense pressure and anguish.[122]

There are, according to Bataille, three modes of continuity available to the discontinuous subject: physical eroticism (commonly understood as sexuality); spiritual eroticism (the experience of the mystic); and death:

Erotic experience linked with reality waits upon chance, upon a particular person and favourable circumstances. Religious eroticism through mystical experience requires only that the subject shall not be disturbed.[123]

Death is the most difficult of the three to avoid:

Assenting to life even in death is a challenge to death, in emotional eroticism as well as physical, a challenge to death through indifference to death. Life is a door into existence: life may be doomed but the continuity of existence is not. The nearness of this continuity and its heady quality are more powerful than the thought of death. To begin with, the first turbulent surge of erotic feeling overwhelms all else, so that gloomy considerations of the fate in store for our discontinuous selves are forgotten. And then, beyond the intoxication of youth, we achieve the power to look death in the face and to perceive in death the pathway into unknowable and incomprehensible continuity – that path is the secret of eroticism and eroticism alone can reveal it.[124]

All forms of eroticism lead to 'the blending and fusion of separate objects ... to eternity ... to death, and through death to continuity.'[125]

Surprisingly, however, Bataille's chosen illustration of fusion turns out to be drawn from *birth* rather than *death*:

> In asexual reproduction, the organism, a single cell, divides at a certain point in its growth. Two nuclei are formed and from one single being two new beings are derived. But we cannot say that one being has given birth to a second being. The first being has disappeared. It is to all intents and purposes dead, in that it does not survive in either of the two beings it has produced. It does not decompose in the way that sexual animals do when they die, but it ceases to exist. It ceases to exist in so far as it was discontinuous. But at one stage of the reproductive process there was continuity. There is a point at which the original *one becomes two*. As soon as there are two, there is again discontinuity for each of the beings. But the process entails *one instant* of continuity between the two of them. The first one dies, but as it dies there is a moment of continuity between the two new beings.

In human sexuality '[t]he same continuity cannot occur in the death of sexual creatures, where reproduction is in theory independent of death and disappearance.' The moment of conception, however, is a primary model of cellular fusion:

> Sperm and ovum are to begin with discontinuous entities, but they *unite*, and consequently a continuity comes into existence between them to form a new entity from the death and disappearance of the separate beings. The new entity is itself discontinuous, but it bears within itself the transition to continuity, the fusion, fatal to both, of two separate beings.[126]

Maryline Lukacher cites this passage in her discussion of Bataille's *My Mother,* suggesting that '[t]he mother's abjection opens the pathway back to extinction and death'.[127] We can extend the correlation between pregnant and maternal subjectivities in a different direction, to consider a potentially conscious apprehension of fusion available to female-embodied experience under certain conditions. Kristeva's work is already influential here, foregrounding the 'importance of the maternal space' against its repeated foreclosure in critical theorizing.[128] Something certainly 'dies' in the transition from daughter to mother. The woman who conceived no longer exists in the same way after the birth of the first child.

There are a number of material and experiential realities related to pregnant embodiment that can be understood through the recognition of the particularity of maternal subjectivities. Iris Marion Young, for example, has claimed the condition of the pregnant subject as 'not simply a splitting in which the two halves lie open and still, but a dialectic'.[129] The pregnant subject transforms into a maternal subject over time. The continuities are striking, as delineated by Janet Martin Soskice. Both the pregnant and the maternal subject are defined by their attendance to 'the new other':

> Whereas before birth the mother's body unreflectively attends to the needs of the embryo, after the birth the brain joins the other organs (kidneys, guts, lungs) in attending to the new other. Or better, the whole active being of the mother, in all her instinctual and reflective capacities, is brought to bear on the needs of the baby.[130]

Fortunately for this argument that 'whole' does not absorb all her conscious and unconscious mind, which can do other things while her organs and limbs attend to the 'new other', like reflect on the experience and even make some notes for future reference.

Bataille's concept of 'fusion' and maternal subjectivity are very close bed partners. Conception, pregnancy, birthing, cutting of the umbilical cord, post-partum release of the placental 'partial object', lactation and primary care for the 'new other' provide a core set of subject-producing processes unavoidably associated with – and attached to – the maternal-feminine body by the embodied consciousness that emerges from this process (all going well). Any experience of 'fusion', then, refers directly to the state of female-embodiment as the remnant of original continuity necessarily discarded by the new other's achievement of discontinuous individuation, which does not occur all at once on arrival in the world. Bataille severely limits his example of 'fusion' by attending only to the momentary flash of continuity experienced by the male partner at conception (no surprises there then). It seems legitimate to extend his thought to consider the fully radiating, and often conscious, 'inner experience' of fusion that is the common condition of pregnancy and of maternal subjectivity more generally. The maternal subject arguably lives in a perpetual state of partial fusion.

Foucault simply may not have noticed that the framework for transgression, the ground against which Bataille's theoretically masculine subject rubs himself into transgression, is female embodiment (in the differentiated forms of the mother, the lover, the prostitute and – of course – GOD). Judith Starkis argues convincingly that Foucault 'appropriates and repositions Bataille's theory' in an attempt 'to lose himself (rupture his own philosophical and discursive limit) in Bataille'. The sum effect is that gender is 'effac[ed]' by Foucault's appropriation.[131]

We would seem to have inherited a mode of critical transgression that has no place for female-embodied experience. Ironic really, given that for Bataille 'the woman, as the marker of difference, becomes the site upon which transgression appears', and 'feminine dissolution is thus necessarily prior to the masculine'. Further, the arch 'masculine' theorist cannot get close to transgression without this intimate encounter with female-embodiment: '[t]he masculine partner in physical eroticism has difficulty sensing transgression within himself'. However, 'descriptions of the woman-subject are remarkably missing from Foucault's discussion'.[132] The implications for Starkis are clear:

> An interrogation of the gendering operative in transgression then raises a number of further questions concerning the radicality of gestures towards self-loss (a series of questions that, in his attempt to proclaim the disruptiveness of transgression, Foucault cannot afford to address.)[133]

Women always come first with Bataille. The illusion of their absence dominates Foucault's thought.

Foucault's 'Preface To Transgression' is now widely recognized and celebrated as a keystone in the structure of feeling that posits 'transgression' against 'dialectic': 'From this point on, theorists will look to transgression as a way of getting beyond the constraints of Hegelian dialectic'.[134] But what's wrong with a little constraint? Constraint, as taboo or interdiction, is for Bataille (as Laure noted) the 'choke-hold that makes you come'. Constraint is the limit that forces the Bataillean 'masculine' subject to experience himself as a bounded being with access to unbounded 'Totality' nonetheless. Constraint, as necessity, is the limit of the discontinuous being and the border that invites transgression. Death is the ultimate constraint to the will to power. Laure, as ever, was sharply aware of this productive contradiction:

To assert yourself as free you need me as your chains. Then there is
something to break, an established order of things to *transgress*. Me, a
little girl behaving with you as my mother with me. I must delay your
pleasures so that they increase tenfold.[135]

Lost in the dizzying notion of liberating constraint and its loss in
liberation, I went looking for a female-embodied transgression
narrative, and found it in that most feminocentric tale of constraint,
Story of O. Now, *Story of O* seems to offer a conscious response to
Bataille's *Story of the Eye*. The titles in French are very similar, the 'O' of
'Oeil' suggesting something of the eye/I slippage available in English.
The roundness of the O corresponds to the egg/saucer of *Eye's* milk/
castrated testicle/eyeball chain of reference, reducing roundness to a
mark of writing. O is also empty/zero/nothing/hole, recalling the
cultural associations of femininity: O is wanting.

Anne Desclos's extraordinary novel was written, under the
pseudonym Pauline Réage, to demonstrate to her lover, Jean Paulhan,
that erotic literature could be produced from the female-embodied
standpoint. She seems, in retrospect, to have won whatever interesting
argument had initiated the work. Published to great controversy in
1954, but awarded the *Prix des Deux Magots* in 1955, *Story of O* offers
an excruciating vision of eroticism from the 'woman's point of view'.
This 'point of view' demonstrates above all else a peculiarly feminine
claim to a mode of liberation achieved through increasing constraint.[136] It captures the possibility of a counterpoint to the sheer
incontinence of critical and narrative transgression in the solely
masculine. It is important to keep in mind during the following
discussion that I am reading *O* in the tradition of feminine narrative
romance rather than as a work of social realism. That is, I am
interested in the way this narrative models liberation for the female-
embodied subject, rather than in the way it 'reflects' the reality of its
context.

The links between *O* and *Eye* are in the first place intellectual:
Jean Paulhan (Desclos's lover and employer, an intellectual publisher
and academic, and first audience) was known to have participated
in Bataille's lecture series at the 'College of Sociology' between
1938–9 (probably alongside Denis de Rougemont, Walter Benjamin,
Adorno and Horkheimer, Lacan).[137] Bataille reviewed the novel
on its publication, where he placed it above Samuel Beckett's
Malloy.[138] Desclos (who wrote criticism as Dominique Aury)
was steeped in de Sade, and Paulhan's commentary on the novel
makes this clear:

> Few are the men who have not dreamt of possessing a Justine. But as best I know no woman has so far dreamt of being Justine.[139]

I like this notion of a reverse-fantasy from poor old Justine's perspective and will use it as a starting point for reflecting on a counter-model to the hyper-masculine mode of transgression that reaches us through the intellectual tradition of Sade-Nietzsche-Bataille-Foucault.

There is between *O* and *Eye* a distinctive intertextual link in Reage's image of a 'fly in a saucer of milk' that compresses both the infamous 'saucer of milk' in which Simone squats and the hideous image of the fly landing on the white of the dead priest's eyeball:

> Little Nathalie had sat down in the white carpet in the middle of the room, poised like a fly in a saucer of milk.[140]

Story of O is aware of Bataille's *Eye*. Susan Sontag's essay on 'The Pornographic Imagination' accounts for both Réage and Bataille's pornographic writings as 'part of the history of art rather than of trash':

> The physical sensations involuntarily produced in someone reading the book carry with them something that touches upon the reader's whole experience of his humanity – and his limits as a personality and as a body ... Pornography is one of the branches of literature – science fiction is another – aiming at disorientation, at psychic dislocation.[141]

Sontag is particularly keen on O's haunting power as a character, her power to confound readerly expectations:

> Although passive, O scarcely resembles those ninnies in Sade's tales who are detained in remote castles to be tormented by pitiless noblemen and satanic priests ... O is represented as active, too: literally active, as in the seduction of Jacqueline, and more important, profoundly active in her own passivity.[142]

O undertakes a *consenting* narrative journey from recognizable, modern woman (she works as a professional photographer) to dehumanized object of the unrestrained desires of others. What is remarkable is that she is represented calmly in the course of this journey towards self-destruction at the hands of others' desires, gradually unfolding towards a happiness in her ultimate objectification previously unattainable to her 'free' self:

Once upon a time she'd been indifferent and fickle, had amused herself tempting the boys who were wild about her, she'd tease them with a word, with a gesture, but never cede an inch … neither her bad-boy's manners, nor the fact she'd had a few lovers … nor her harshness, nor even her courage had been of the least service to her when she'd met René. In the space of a week she became acquainted with fear, but with certitude also, with anguish, but also with happiness. René leapt at her throat like a corsair springing upon a captive, and, deliciously, she became captivated, at her wrists, at her ankles, all over her limbs and far down within her heart's and body's secrete recesses feeling tied by bonds subtler, more invisible than the finest hair, stronger than the cables wherewith the Lilliputians made Gulliver prisoner, bonds her lover would tighten or loosen with a glance. She was no longer free? Ah! Thank God no, she wasn't any longer free. But she was buoyant, a cloud-dwelling goddess, a swift-swimming fish of the deeps, but deep-dwelling, forever doomed to happiness.[143]

The novel begins with O driven to the remote chateaux of Roissy by her lover, where she is prostituted to a brotherhood given over to the pursuit of unrestrained sexual pleasure:

He told her that she belonged, and was ultimately answerable to him, only to him, even if she were to receive orders from others than he, no matter whether he were there or absent … that it was he who possessed and enjoyed her through the agency of those into whose hands he surrendered her, and this was so from the mere fact that she was surrendered to them by him, she was the gift, he the donor … Thus he would possess her as a god possessed his creatures whereupon he lays hands guised as some monster or bird, as some invisible spirit or as ecstacy itself … The fact he gave her to others was proof … that she belonged to him. He gave her so as to have her immediately back, and recovered her enriched a hundredfold in his eyes, as is an ordinary object that has served some divine purpose and thereby become infused with sanctity.[144]

The rococo language of the sacred here is key to O's narrative location. Her bondage is experienced subjectively as a release from the burden of her ordinary self to a freedom through objectification: 'She heard a voice declare that she ought to be made to kneel, and she was. It was painful to be on her knees, seated on her heels in the position nuns take when they pray'.[145]

It is a natural, common-sense response to be outraged by O's treatment and objectification at the service of the outrageous pleasures of others. O herself is serene in the midst of the anguish of her humiliation and bodily torture:

The chains and the silence which ought to have sealed her isolated self within twenty impenetrable walls, to have asphyxiated her, strangled her, hadn't; to the contrary, they'd been her deliverance, liberating her from herself. What might have become of her had speech been accorded her and freedom granted her hands, had the faculty of free will been hers when her lover prostituted her while he looked on? ... she sank, lost in a delirious absence from herself which gave her unto love and loving, and may perhaps have brought her close to death and dying.[146]

The despoiling of her person is transformed – again subjectively – into a sanctification:

> Daily and, as it were, ritualistically soiled by saliva and sperm, by sweat mingled with her own sweat, she sensed herself to be, literally, the vessel of impurity, the gutter whereof Scripture makes mention. And yet in all those parts of her body which were the most continually offended, having become more sensitive, seemed to her to have become, at the same time, more lovely, and as though ennobled ... However astonishing it were, that from being prostituted her dignity may increase, the crucial point was nonetheless one of dignity. It illumined her from within, and one could see her calmness in her bearing, upon her countenance the serenity and imperceptible inner smile one rather guesses at than perceives in the eyes of the recluse.[147]

Finally the muted association between the worldly agency of her lover and the divine agency of a 'living god' is made explicit. As a child she'd read a text written in letters of red upon the white wall of a room she'd spent two months living in:

> 'It is a terrible thing to fall into the hands of the living God.' No, she said to herself, no, it isn't true. What is terrible is to be rejected by the hands of the living God.[148]

Sontag notes that *O* 'unfolds ... a spiritual paradox, that of the full void and of the vacuity that is also a plenum'.[149] It is a useful paradox, in that it reveals the structural convergence of femininity and emptiness. The novel's power 'lies exactly in the anguish stirred up by the continuing presence of this paradox.' The most disturbing (psychically dislocating) phase of *O* comes in the last chapter of the novel, in which she is finally dehumanized to the point of becoming an animal or dead object: 'in the vision of the world presented by *Story of O*, the highest good is the transcendence of personality'.[150] This is also the most significant in terms of any possible analysis. O's journey to selflessness is a narrative account of what we might call abstract femininity. Anne Carolyn Klein has noted that the spiritual tradition of 'the wisdom of selflessness' has long been 'characterized as female'.[151] *O* can be read as a romance narrative following the subject's final attainment of 'emptiness' (Bataille's 'continuity' or ultimate liberation) achieved through an extreme capitulation to a mode of femininity foreclosed by more common sense or materialist models of liberation.

Branded with the initials of her new 'owner', scarred by whipping, naked and chained by an iron ring attached to her labia, O is given a choice of masks to wear:

> Nathalie returned with the carton. She put it upon the bed. She opened it and, one by one, took out and removed from their paper wrappings the objects it contained, and handed them one after another to Sir Stephen. They were masks. They were head-dresses and masks at the same time, they were intended to cover the entire head, everything except the eyes – there were two holes for the eyes – and the mouth and chin. All sorts of masks: sparrow-hawk, falcon, owl, fox, lion, bull, but only animal masks, scaled to human proportions . . . O tried on each of the masks. The most curious of them all, and the one which simultaneously transformed her the most and seemed the most natural to her, was one of the owl-masks.[152]

Not any animal then, but specifically the 'owl' is chosen by and for O to frame her final experience of dehumanization. O's narrative journey is from recognizably contemporary professional (liberated) woman through consenting scenes of sexual subjection, to slavery (objectification), costumed as an owl, in chains, exposed to the gaze and touch of any who come across her. In the alternative ending that follows the words 'The End' she is imagined dead:

> There existed another ending to the story of O. Seeing herself about to be left by Sir Stephen, she preferred to die. To which he gave his consent.[153]

The owl as a structural equivalent to death is a significant figure for this discussion. Bataille draws on the owl in his account of the man of history:

> As for what is exclusively mine, I have only described my existence after it has reached a definite stance. When I speak of recognition of the 'man of recognized negativity', I speak of the state of my requirements now: description only comes afterward. It seems to me that until then Minerva can hear the owl.[154]

Bataille takes the figure of Minerva's owl from Hegel's famous image, in his preface to the *Philosophy of Right* (1821):

> One more word about giving instruction as to what the world ought to be. Philosophy in any case always comes on the scene too late to give it . . . When philosophy paints its gray in gray, then has a shape of life

> grown old. By philosophy's gray in gray it cannot be rejuvenated but
> only understood. The owl of Minerva spreads its wings only with the
> falling of the dusk.

According to Peter Singer, 'Minerva, the Roman goddess of wisdom,
was the equivalent of the Greek goddess Athena. She was associated
with the owl, traditionally regarded as wise, and hence a metaphor for
philosophy ... [h]e meant that philosophy understands reality only
after the event. It cannot prescribe how the world ought to be'.[155] Yes,
but is it not also significant that to a female divinity the owl speaks its
late wisdom?

The owl that O becomes by subjecting herself to the harsh
determinants of her lover's extreme desire, then, is not just a figure
of obscene femininity as the animalized, dehumanized, object of an
alien and brutalizing will. Minerva's owl, embodied by O in the scene
of her final humiliation, prefigures the final negation of the negation of
nature: achieved by the feminine subject *in spite of* her humanity, at the
literal expense of those who inflict their will upon her. O offers an
allegorical narrative of the feminine subject as a negative mode of
passive agency within structures of oppressive determinacy; always
already a Hegelian slave, but freed by the power to consent to her
determination. The forked beginning and ending of O's narrative
offers a plurality and plenitude in answer to Bataille's searing erotics
of the blissful *expenditure* of male-embodied subjectivity. O might
stand for the sacred Owl of Minerva, mythical aspect of the Goddess of
wisdom and war, taking flight in the darkness at the dusk of
Enlightenment, when dreams of progress through reason have fallen
into the instrumentalization of industrial capital.

Hegel's owl flew at the end of the decade that saw the coming into
consciousness of Austen's *Persuasion* (1818): a narrative charting the
eternal return of history at the level of the feminine subject of desire.
The critical lateness of the return of the object in *Persuasion* marks the
moment when feminine desire becomes finally conscious of itself,
when all seems already to have been lost. What returns, against all
odds, is love itself:

> All the privilege I claim for my own sex (it is not a very enviable one,
> you need not covet it) is that of loving longest, when existence or when
> hope is gone.[156]

It's a cool analysis, but what does it mean? Minerva's Owl seems
to capture something of the recognition that human reason works

retrospectively. In the daylight of the weaving of reality the owl sleeps; at twilight she takes flight and sees what has been done while she slept. Like the emergent properties of the wasp's nest, human endeavour is never *really* fully conscious, except as the expression of unmediated desire, but can subsequently (once the forces at work in the construction are past, and we no longer desire except nostalgically) be taken as a dense and condensed object of formal knowledge. The Owl of Minerva is the figure of a particular mode of knowing, one associated with the end of light, able to pierce the darkness and take wing. The Owl flies as Enlightenment darkens into the shadows of Blake's 'Satanic Mills'; or in the evening when the rational identities of day-time work are put aside for the more private pleasures of the evening and night.

We are given a reference to the 'later eighteenth century' as the context for this figure of historical consciousness, which is also a conscious reference for O's paradoxical feminine subjectivity, helpfully encountered through her reflection in a mirror:

> O, standing up in front of the bow-legged bureau she used as a dressing-table, and above which she saw herself from head to waist in the antique mirror, a little greenish, or mossy, as though submarine, that image ... it made her think of those engravings dating from the later eighteenth century, engravings showing women wandering naked in the subdued light of their apartments, in the height of the summer's heat.[157]

The 'later eighteenth century' takes us back to the immediate context for de Sade's writings, the closure of the dreams of rational Enlightenment in the darkness of the Terror, and the dawn of a recognizably modern feminism through Mary Wollstonecraft's surge into writing. The 'later eighteenth century' finally – as Sontag notes – denotes the historical 'loss' of an accessible experience of totality:

> Perhaps the deepest spiritual resonance of the career of pornography in its 'modern' Western phase under consideration here ... is this vast frustration of human passion and seriousness since the old religious imagination, with its secure monopoly on the total imagination, began in the late eighteenth century to crumble. ... Most pornography ... points to something more general than even sexual damage. I mean the traumatic failure of modern capitalist society to provide authentic outlets for the perennial human flair for high-temperature visionary obsessions, to satisfy the appetite for exalted self-transcending modes of concentration and seriousness. The need of human beings to transcend 'the personal' is no less profound than the need to be a person.[158]

The 'female point of view' narrated as the obscene femininity of *Story of O* is represented differently in the narrative of the 'Eye', which makes its way through an obscenely feminized landscape immersed in ovular roundness and liquification. Pornography is ultimately obscene, as Bataille's intelligent narrative pornography witnesses, because it foregrounds female materiality and its particular powers of affectation. It is obscene in a way that refers to its direct relation to the sacred. Bataille's *Eye* is displaced from the head of the priest, where it occupies a place of ocular power or judgement. It is first shaded by the grill of the confession, then dragged into the light, turned back in horror at what it is forced to witness, and finally violently displaced to occupy an otherwise unimaginable perspective of defiled sight. It is not a coincidence, nor merely a terrible thought, to resituate the knowing eye of the priest (symbolic of Christian epistemology) in the cunt of a heroine of feminine defilement. The blue weeping eye has migrated from the masculine, spiritual head to the specifically female, material bottom: not bisexually situated but collapsing entirely the top/bottom, mind/body, male/female, seeing/seen, subject/object dualism.

This may be the point that Foucault did not want to see; then again, this was not a place he was inclined to look. Perhaps as a result, Foucault's 'Preface' takes transgression at face value: as if it testified to 'the limit' that could and should be perpetually overrun, until there is no land and only sea; no form, only endless, libidinal movement. We might rather conclude that the *Eye* (as privileged subject of sight, knowledge, perception, ocular and occidental power) now gazes back from a different place. This thought is anguished and queasy in the way that any disturbance to the conditions of sight would make the subject of the gaze anguished and queasy, at least temporarily. After a bit of practice it is possible to see again without feeling nauseous. 'As a man is, so he sees; as the eye is formed, such are its powers'.[159]

3

'A Serious and Dangerous Matter': Transgression and the Death of God

A Few Words concerning Conscience, what it is, and what estate it was in before transgression. And how it became darkened . . . and corrupted. And how it may be enlightened . . . and set at liberty, etc. (William Shewen, 1675)

Remember that the world has suffered because it believed it saw the light extinguished that keeps God, alive and in peace, on earth. It will only shine again in your youthful desires. Peace is not a weary, heavy sleep after the storm: it is awakening to life and to all its beauty, to goodness, for you will love with new ardour. You will love our Lord because he has loved you so much he gave his blood for you so that your hope would not falter in suffering. And you will love one another, because mankind has suffered too much for having forgotten how to love each other.[160] (Bataille)

Really, a young Atheist cannot guard his faith too carefully. Dangers lie in wait for him on every side.[161] (C.S. Lewis)

Transgression has quite a history, then. Leaving aside for a moment its place in human expulsion from Edenic consciousness, in Bataille's intellectual career the concept is explored at most length in *Eroticism*

[1957]. In Foucault's, the concept is taken up in 'Preface to Transgression' only 6 years later. Paul Hegarty stresses that transgression, following Bataille, is in the *writing itself* and its capacity to raise and perform the idea of transgression.[162] The tradition of critical transgression takes the act of *writing itself*, then, as a peculiar cultural space where significant things can happen. *Story of the Eye* is in the first instance transgressive as a piece of published and critically acknowledged narrative writing (a funny thing to come across in a University library). But as Hegarty rather sheepishly notes, this mode of transgression is not *really* all that novel or radical:

> Arguably, the use of pornography as a genre subverts the criteria of philosophy, both in terms of content and in terms of reader-response. But some would raise the question of the validity of such an approach, arguing that 'philosophical porn' is the ultimate in male exploitative writing, allowing pornography into higher culture.

Transgression, it seems, is an inconceivably old idea writ new. We cannot simply shake it off. Bataille's persistent return to archaic societies and their more organized, one might say more rational, approach to transgression as a rigorous, collective encounter with the sacred (through sacrifice, carnival, marriage) has diminished to Foucault's dreary account of the contemporary (post-war Europe) as a time of 'profanation without an object':

> profanation in a world which no longer recognizes any positive meaning in the sacred – is this not more or less what we call transgression?[163]

For Foucault, transgression is simply unavoidable in a world steeped in 'the death of God'. Not God's absence, but the insistence on his death, is the primary condition for the thought of transgression. Bataille's body of work and Foucault's 'Preface' are almost entirely preoccupied by the critical and ethical implications of thinking the 'death of God':

> Perhaps the importance of sexuality in our culture, the fact that since Sade it has persistently been linked to the most profound decisions of our language, derives from nothing else than this correspondence which connects it to the death of God.

Sexuality in the context of 'the death of God' is the core of Foucault's model of transgression. He goes on to specify what he means by 'the death of God' and its implications for Bataille's work:

> Not that this death should be understood as the end of his historical reign or as the finally delivered judgement of his non-existence, but as the now constant space of our experience ... Bataille was perfectly conscious of the possibilities of thought that could be released by this death, and of the impossibilities in which it entangled thought.

The 'death of God' is not a simple idea, however, and certainly not one to be taken lightly:

> What, indeed, is the meaning of the death of God, if not a strange solidarity between the stunning realization of his non-existence and the act that kills him? But what does it mean to kill God if he does not exist, to kill God *who has never existed*?'[164]

What indeed... The 'act' that kills God is an act of mind; a 'realization'. The death of God that is the intellectual context for the thought of transgression from the late 18th century onwards is a creative thought, or at least the decision to rest with that thought. It is a thought concretized in the frenzy of decapitation that symbolized the forces of the French Revolution and its intellectual heritage: Bataille's Acéphalic movement was symbolized by the headless man. Since God is an idea, the death of God is only a thought, and one that arises in different ways at different times. Critical thought is now in danger of wallowing in transgression in painful consciousness of its complicity in 'killing' God. It may no longer be possible to avoid the contemporary thought that is the death of God but it is perhaps possible to think the death of God, and therefore the critical terrain of transgression, differently.

A trawl through the British Library catalogue gives us a useful snapshot of the publishing history of transgression as a concept. The first open reference to transgression in the title of a published work listed in the BL catalogue dates from 1595, with Daniel Drouin's comprehensively titled *Les Vengéances divines de la transgression des sainctes ordannances de Dieu, selon l'ordre des dix commandemens*. Five further references emerge in the 17th century, all of which understand transgression as the act that produces a state of sin, the fall from grace (see the Appendix for full details). The 18th century shows a decline, with only two published works registering the word in the title. The 19th century sees a gentle rise, perhaps in line with the proportional rise of published works, with eight explicit claims to transgression in the title of published works, one of which is Zola's *Abbé Mouret's Transgression, A realist novel* (published in London in 1886). It is in the

20th century that the concept proliferates; but only eleven published titles use it between 1900 and 1981. Then there are thirteen in the 1980s, 48 in the 1990s, and 42 *to date* in the new millennium (at least 43 by the time you read this).

The framing of transgression has shifted drastically in this avalanche of writing, from a concern with the implications of the human fall from Grace, towards a preoccupation with materiality, the body, sexuality and death. Foucault famously foregrounded sexuality as the key to the era of critical transgression:

> What characterizes modern sexuality from Sade to Freud is not its having found the language of its logic or of its natural process, but rather, through the violence done by such languages, its having been 'denatured' – cast into an empty zone where it achieves whatever meagre form is bestowed upon it by the establishment of its limits. Sexuality points to nothing beyond itself, no prolongation, except in a frenzy which disrupts it. We have not in the least liberated sexuality, though we have, to be exact, carried it to its limits.[165]

The most interesting development in transgression, however, is the way the concept now increasingly operates as an *academic* term. It also has a far wider range of associations and uses: recent titles freely attach the notion of transgression to fashion, angels, interior design and extreme metal music. The most remarkable shift in the history of transgression as a concept is the one that blithely resituates it from a mistake of cosmic proportions towards an affirmative social activity: *Celebrating Transgression: method and politics in anthropological studies of culture* (Rao and Hutnyk, 2006).

To celebrate transgression properly, as Philippe Sollers has already argued, we are obliged to affirm the prohibitions that make transgression possible in the first place:

> Therefore the difficulty is this: since the word 'transgression' tends to efface the 'prohibition' (in a society where the notion of prohibition is practically invisible), we must begin by reaffirming prohibition.[166]

Arguing for transgression without attending to its basis in prohibition, according to Sollers, leads us to the despair of a 'pseudo-transgression' where 'the resulting "liberation" is no more than the mask for a redoubled repression'.[167] This is an important point. Prohibitions make us desire to go beyond them: 'The prohibition is there to be violated'.[168] The violation highlights and reinstates the prohibition rather than erasing it. What is at stake here is the nature of 'prohibition': an arbitrary social construction associated with 'oppression', or something pre-existing social and cultural forms and only partially expressed through them? The former understanding of prohibition justifies transgression, in fact must sanction and encourage it in the name of liberational social progress. The latter, prohibition as foundational taboo, makes one stop and think a little about the compulsion to transgress. To make this less abstract, consider your own experience of reaching the age of sexual consent. Did you wait like a good citizen for that moment before you started to explore sexual relations with others, or did you rather see it as a deadline? The age of sexual consent has a particular effect of eroticising under-sixteens as prohibited objects of sexual desire while offering abstract legal protection to them. As a mother of daughters I have to wonder to what extent it is the prohibition that creates the erotic charge for transgression. As a daughter reaching for 16, I experienced that prohibition as an arbitrary constraint on my natural rights.

Let's face it: active, multiple, casual sexual relations are now normal among teenagers across Western Europe, were already normative in my own adolescence. Our young women *are* largely liberated from the biological implications of heterosexual relations by increasing access to contraception and abortion rights since the 1960s. The fact that the most economically disadvantaged tend to overlook the pragmatics of contraception has not yet been processed in discourses of transgression. Free Love is still an economic idea above all else, and one that greases the circulation of interchangeable bodies in mass economies of desire and despair: 'an unblocked, liberated, free-flowing, machine desire is a very accommodating, if not ideal, force, or subject, of consumer capitalism'.[169] I recently overheard a conversation among some strikingly well-dressed students while queuing at a cash point. The conversation involved an absent female friend fondly known as 'The Slag', who was 'up for anything' and 'with anyone'. One of the conversants (who were happy to be over-heard based on their unabashed volume) seemed bemused that this friend had recently got a bit 'upset' when a joke was made in her presence that involved the leg of an upturned stool.

What ideas have we left to offer our young as coordinates by which to negotiate their own becoming as sexuate individuals? Having achieved transgression of traditional sexual prohibitions at least a generation ago, post-16 girls in the West now have little reason (aside from taste, which is fickle and thrives on exploration) to avoid sexual contact:

> With the absence of God, with morality no longer obeisant to a spiritual form, we achieve profanation without object. The Godless vocabulary of modern sexuality achieves limits and prescribes ends in the place previously held by the infinite.[170]

There is evidence of the effect of a 'Godless vocabulary of sexuality' in modern confessional narratives of sexual heroinism, epitomized by Catherine Millet's *The Sexual Life of Catherine M* (2001). The genre continues to sell, as evidenced by Catherine Townsend's *Sleeping Around: secrets of a sexual adventuress* (2007):

> Some people are horrified by women admitting to the hedonistic pursuit of pleasure for its own sake. Yet most of my male friends seem to think that they will sleep around and have adventures until the right girl comes along. So why should women be any different?[171]

It is a good question. Any hint of calling on traditional 'morality' to answer it would probably invite transgression in the name of liberation:

> The problematics for post-structuralism, and the 'post-' more generally, have been set and transgression has been revealed as both an intellectual implement and a life-enhancing practice. The sovereign survivor in the postmodern culture is compelled to transgress.[172]

That a critical mass of us now know by experience and reflection that this polymorphous fantasy soon gives way in practice to a sticky ritual of repetitive bodily acts that promise but permanently withhold transcendence should make some difference to this debate. Robert Hughes notes in his recent personal retrospective on London in the 1960s:

> I am glad that I never bought into the 'fuck-and-you-shall-be-free' ideology that was so common in London and elsewhere at the time. I sensed then, and know with a fair degree of certainty now, that it is an illusion to suppose that sexual promiscuity helps create personal freedom. There is a huge difference between the condition of freedom and that of accepting no responsibilities to anyone.[173]

Even Georges Bataille, who celebrated the potential for a radical experience of continuity by the non-continuous being in abstract erotic encounters, grew to acknowledge that

> [w]ithout the intimate understanding between two bodies that only grows with time conjunction is furtive and superficial, unorganized,

practically animal and far too quick ... A taste for constant change is certainly neurotic.[174]

It is possible that what we now need to offer our young (and ourselves) is simply the right, and the conditions, to wait and see. The literary evidence alone, however, suggests that we are on the slippery slide towards generational sexual overload, directly related to the 'death of God' and the condition of transgression this thought has engendered. Catherine Millet's libertinism is forged in the mould of her earlier Catholicism, her passivity, and her inability to find a good enough reason *not to*:

> Even if I have kept some of the reflexes of a practising Catholic to this day (secretly making the sign of the cross if I'm afraid something is going to happen ...), I can no longer really pretend that I believe in God. It's quite possible that I lost this belief when I started having sexual relationships. Finding myself vacant, then, with no other mission to fulfil, I grew into a rather passive woman, having no goal other than those that other people set for me ... As I was completely available, I sought no more ideals in love than I did in my professional life, I was seen as someone who had no taboos, someone exceptionally uninhibited, and I had no reason not to fill this role.[175]

This sounds to me very much like giving in.

Critical transgression emerges from the thought of the death of God, and this thought has as one of its characteristics a necessary dismissal of morality (the word itself hangs heavy on my computer screen). Nietzsche's iconic madman rampages through the collective minds of the academy:

> The madman jumped into their midst and pierced them with his eyes. 'Whither is God?' he cried; 'I will tell you. *We have killed him* – you and I. All of us are his murderers. But how did we do this? How could we drink up the sea? Who gave us the sponge to wipe away the entire horizon? What were we doing when we unchained this earth from its sun? Whither is it moving now? Whither are we moving? Away from all suns? Are we plunging continuously? Backward, sideward, forward, in all directions? Is there still any up or down? Are we not straying as though through an infinite nothing? Do we not feel the breath of empty space? Has it not become colder? Is not night continually closing in on us? Do we not need to light lanterns in the morning? Do we hear nothing as yet of the noise of the gravediggers who are burying God? Do we smell nothing as yet of the divine decomposition? Gods, too, decompose. God remains dead. And we have killed him.'[176]

'God' had in fact already died at least once before. Thoughts of the 'death of God' saturate the discourse of transgression from the 1790s onwards. In the English tradition, P.B. Shelley had argued coolly that since

> it is evident that having no proofs from any of the three sources of conviction: the mind *cannot* believe the existence of a God, it is also evident that as belief is a passion of the mind, no degree of criminality can be attached to disbelief, they only are reprehensible who willingly neglect to remove the false medium thro' which their mind views the subject.[177]

The Marquis de Sade had also noted the necessity of atheism to a man of reason:

> As we gradually proceeded to our enlightenment, we came more and more to feel that, motion being inherent in matter, the prime mover existed only as an illusion, and that all that exists having to be in motion, the motor was useless; we sensed that this chimerical divinity, prudently invented by the earliest legislators, was, in their hands, simply one more means to enthrall us, and that, reserving unto themselves the right to make the phantom speak they knew very well how to get him to say nothing but what would shore up the preposterous laws whereby they declared they served us.[178]

Nick Land quotes this extraordinarily prescient point in de Sade on the way to declaring his own mode of post-Christianity:

> There is only one sane and healthy relation to Christianity; perfect indifference. Mine is not of that kind. My detestation for the Christian faith exhausts my being, and more. I long for its God to exist in order to slake myself as violence upon him. If there are torments coming to me I want them, all of them; God experimenting in cruelty upon me. I want no lethargy in Hell, rather vigour and imagination. Oh yes, it is all very wretched, and if I am grateful to Christianity it is for one thing alone; it has taught me how to *hate*.[179]

It is indeed terrible to be 'abandoned by the living God'; a stern word is better than indifference. Transgression might only be looking to provoke some scrap of evidence of a still-living God, in the way that an older sibling plays up to earn the gaze of an otherwise distracted parent.

Bataille had converted to Catholicism against the backdrop of his own father's syphilitic death. He never really left the structuring beliefs of Christianity behind: his transgressions were *always* in the eyes of his God. Even Surya suggests that Bataille was 'never definitively an atheist'.[180] He was never really a materialist either:

> Communication, through death, with our beyond (essentially in sacrifice) – not with nothingness, still less with a supernatural being, but with an indefinite reality (which I sometimes call the *impossible*, that is: what can't be grasped in any way, what we can't reach without dissolving ourselves, what's slavishly called God). If we need to we can define this reality (provisionally associating it with a finite element) at a higher (higher than the individual on the scale of composition of beings) social level as the sacred, God or created reality. Or else it can remain in an undefined state (in ordinary laughter, infinite laughter, or ecstasy in which the divine form melts like sugar in water).[181]

The death of God is not a particularly new idea, then, but one that seems to arise in human thought to mark a modal shift; the 'death' of one way of life (mode) that dovetails with the inauguration of another. A new God rises as a central point of community, eventually dies with the culture it coalesces, and arises differently; evidence of the endlessly creative relationship between mind and world, between minds. William Blake's *Songs* mark this transition with more sense of style than de Sade's monotonous prose. The 'Divine Image' of human potential captured in 'Innocence' in 1793 associates the virtues of humanity with a present, creative God:

> To Mercy Pity Peace and Love
> All pray in their distress:
> And to these virtues of delight
> Return their thankfulness.
>
> For Mercy Pity Peace and Love,
> Is God our father dear;
> And Mercy Pity Peace and Love,
> Is Man his child and care.
>
> For Mercy has a human heart
> Pity, a human face:
> And Love, the human form divine,
> And Peace, the human dress.
>
> Then every man of every clime,
> That prays in his distress,
> Prays to the human form divine
> Love Pity Mercy Peace.
>
> And all must love the human form,
> In heathen, turk or jew.
> Where Mercy, Love & Pity dwell,
> There God is dwelling too.[182]

This vision of the human scope for 'Mercy Pity Peace and Love' sinks from its origins in the Divine toward its negation in the absence of the

Divine in a version of the poem apparently written for, but excised from, 'Experience' in 1794:

> Cruelty has a Human Heart
> And Jealousy a Human Face
> Terror, the Human Form Divine
> And Secrecy, the Human Dress
>
> The Human Dress, is forged Iron
> The Human Form, a fiery Forge.
> The Human face, a furnace seal'd
> The Human Heart, its hungry Gorge.[183]

For Blake, the death of God took place in the mind, as a thought that can always be thought, the thinking of which has strong effects on our experience of ourselves and the world. For transgression theory, the death of God has become a rather fixed idea of bland certainty and universality: the death of God everywhere and to all peoples. This is a new aberration in the collective mind of the West: we might have killed the thought of God for our own purposes, but why inflict this thought on the rest of life? Why not, rather, accept that the beardy, white, paradoxically male-embodied Western God of a concrete tradition has died to us, here and now, and then follow through the full implications of that thought?

Sollers comes close to this:

> We are undoubtedly in a dying world – we are that decadent and dying repetition; and thus death has much to tell us, here, today, in this ageing, saturated, closed time.[184]

The dying God is hard-core myth, from Osiris to Tezcatlipoca:

> The accumulated misfortunes and sins of the whole people are sometimes laid upon the dying god, who is supposed to bear them away for ever, leaving the people innocent and happy.[185]

We can find echoes of Frazer's anthropological analysis in the English and French Revolutions, where a re-ordering of material and social reality demanded the sacrifice of the figure of a King-God. In all cases documented by Frazer, the death of God is always a serious matter, a primal ritual performed to purify and strengthen the divine spirit and renew the collective:

> The killing of the god, that is, of his human incarnation, is therefore merely a necessary step to his revival or resurrection in a better form.

> Far from being an extinction of the divine spirit, it is only the begin-
> ning of a purer and stronger manifestation of it.[186]

The 'death' of the God of Christian belief – or at least his dwindling to
a minor deity of a particular tribe – is evidence of a significant
transition in the life of the West, rather than of a new realism that has
finally debunked the superstitions of spiritual belief. There will be new
Gods to discover. Yet it has to be said that the Christian God, however
often and insistently His death has been proclaimed, never seems to
stay very dead. Nick Land still feels the need to stick the critical
knife in:

> I wiped the blade against my jeans and walked into the bar. It was mid-
> afternoon, very hot and still. The bar was deserted. I ordered a whiskey.
> The barman looked at the blood and asked:
> 'God?'
> 'Yeah.'
> 'S'pose it's time someone finished that hypocritical little punk, always
> bragging about his old man's power . . .'
> 'Yeah, I've killed him, knifed the life out of him, once I started I got
> frenzied, it was an ecstasy, I never knew I could hate so much.'[187]

The latest round in this dialectic of belief has been renewed by the
phenomenon of Richard Dawkins' fascinating best-seller, *The God
Delusion* (2006). Perhaps more interesting than the book itself, which
engages intelligent, common-sense materialism and a strong confidence in the theory of evolution as arguments against the persistent
irrationality of religious belief, is the effect it has had on erstwhile
hard-core materialists. Dawkins' tone is of the exasperated realist who
has lost his patience with the romancers of religion. Terry Eagleton's
response in the *London Review of Books* is more lyrical:

> God is an artist who did it for the sheer hell of it, not a scientist at work
> on a magnificently rational design that will impress his research grant
> body no end . . . God is not an obstacle to our autonomy and enjoyment
> but, as Aquinas argues, the power that allows us to be ourselves. Like
> the unconscious, he is closer to us than we are to ourselves. He is the
> source of our self-determination, not the erasure of it. To be dependent
> on him, as to be dependent on our friends, is a matter of freedom and
> fulfilment.[188]

Eagleton then notes, with a tinge of regret, that '[m]ost reasoning
people these days will see excellent grounds to reject . . . the richest,
most enduring form of popular culture in human history'. That
rejection is now an unacknowledged critical orthodoxy, signposted by

'Transgression'. After all, Dawkins' book is not really intended for the intellectual reader – who could be assumed to agree with him already – but for more vulgar minds, not yet disciplined out of the slightest thought of the possibility of God.

Karen Armstrong has argued that the idea of the 'death of God' needs to be properly historicized to prevent it becoming yet another myth:

> There have been many theories about the origin of religion. Yet it seems that creating gods is something that human beings have always done. When one religious idea ceases to work for them, it is simply replaced. These ideas disappear quietly, like the Sky God, with no great fanfare. In our own day, many people would say that the God worshipped for centuries by Jews, Christians, and Muslims has become as remote as the Sky God. Some have actually claimed that he has died. Certainly he seems to be disappearing from the lives of an increasing number of people, especially in Western Europe.[189]

More interesting for this discussion, Armstrong predates the critical thought of transgression with a *literary* death of God:

> It must be significant that after *Paradise Lost* no other major English creative writer would attempt to describe the supernatural world. There would be no more Spensers and Miltons. Henceforth the supernatural and the spiritual would become the domain of more marginal writers, such as C.S. Lewis.[190]

Or of critical theorists like Bataille? This small point may be more significant than it at first appears. Bataille's work engages the very same field of representation, the same questions of the problem of evil and the sacred, the same preoccupation with the presence and absence of divine power, as Lewis's 'marginal' and excessively popular fables. *The Lion, the Witch and the Wardrobe* was published in 1951, in the same decade as Bataille's *Madame Edwarda* (1956).

A sketch of the authors' lives offer some interesting parallels. Born within a year of each other, Bataille and Lewis had experienced as young men the extreme devastation of two European wars. They theorized their way through the collective hallucinations of Nazism, Fascism and Communism as these had come to crystallize and violently reorganize the world they knew. Both had served in the trenches of the First World War, where they had survived the devastation of a generation of men. Lewis carried a piece of shrapnel on his lung as a reminder. Both reflected and wrote their way through the turbulence of the first half of Europe's 20th century, while holding productive and respectable posts in institutions of learning (Lewis was an academic, Bataille a librarian). Both were trained medievalists, with interests in philology. The younger of two brothers, both suffered the loss of a parent in a way that coloured their future writing. Bataille's conversion to Catholicism occurred in the year of his father's death; Lewis also converted to Christianity in the wake of his father's death. Bataille and Lewis considered more seriously than most the question of the sacred in a profane world, and both did this partly in theory, partly in narrative and partly in practice. Both were preoccupied, in mutually informing ways, with the power of transgression.

Maybe this is inevitable. Take any two well-educated, passionately intelligent European men born at the dawn of the 20th century, and you would find similar concerns. Literature itself is always either for or against transgression, it is never neutral on this point. Narratives *either* tell of the reward of good deeds and the punishment of transgression, *or* they posit a world in which a fundamental order has been overturned or inverted. Maybe this point comes down to the simple question of which you would rather read, *Madame Edwarda* or *The Lion, the Witch and the Wardrobe*. In which do you find something of the truth? Both tell the tale of an obscene, alien and crazed femininity and the dissolute chaos it engenders. Both works dislocate the reader's experience of a 'normal' reality, engaging with fantasy to allow for a new encounter with the extraordinary 'real'. Lewis' narrative has a far wider readership and a stronger hold on the popular imagination, but Bataille's remains critically respected as a sharp tool of intellectual transgression. Both can produce the effect of welling tears in the same reader. Lewis addressed this continuum between pleasure and pain, eros and grief:

> Pleasure, pushed to its extreme, shatters us like pain. The longing for a union which only the flesh can mediate while the flesh, our mutually excluding bodies, renders it forever unattainable, can have the grandeur of a metaphysical pursuit. Amorousness as well as grief can bring tears to our eyes.[191]

But what does literature really have to do with transgression? Literature, now largely understood as 'fiction', plays with possibles at the level of the imagination. Perhaps this is why the Humanities have declined as far and as fast as they have; because we have realized that the human sciences 'do' nothing in the world, change nothing, not even minds.[192] Science can change minds as it can change the relationship between elements, reorganize the genetic matrix, increase the harvest. These things cannot be achieved by a novel, by a poem, or even by 'theory'. Houellebecq imagines the end of humanity as an uncomfortably close future for the West:

> The global ridicule inspired by the works of Foucault, Lacan, Derrida and Deleuze, after decades of reverence, far from leaving the field clear for new ideas, simply heaped contempt on all those who were active in 'human sciences'. The rise to dominance of the scientific community in many fields of thought became inevitable.[193]

Bataille found in literature the secular repository for 'extreme states', historically organized through religion:

> But literature only continues the game of religions, of which it is the principal heir. Above all, it has received sacrifice as a legacy: at the start, this longing to lose, to lose ourselves and to look death in the face, found in the ritual of sacrifice, a satisfaction it still gets from the reading of novels. In a sense, sacrifice was a novel, a fictional tale illustrated in a bloody manner ... it is the narrative of a crime whose final episode is *performed* for the spectators by the priest and victim.[194]

Lewis's 'Christianity and Literature' stands in direct opposition to Bataille's 'Literature and Evil'.[195] Lewis is aware that his Christian faith gives him a 'discordant' perspective on the emerging mainstream of late 20th-century critical thought:

> I found a disquieting contrast between the whole circle of ideas used in modern criticism and certain ideas recurrent in the New Testament. Let me say at once it is hardly a question of logical contradiction between clearly defined concepts. It is too vague for that. It is more a repugnance of atmospheres, a discordance of notes, an incompatibility of temperaments.
>
> What are the key words of modern criticism? *Creative*, with its opposite *derivative*; *spontaneity*, with its opposite *convention*; *freedom*, contrasted with *rules*. Great authors are innovators, pioneers, explorers; bad authors bunch in schools and follow models. Or again, great authors are always 'breaking fetters' and 'bursting bonds'. They have personality, they 'are themselves'. I do not know whether we often think through the implications of such language.[196]

Bataille's *Madame Edwarda* now has a serious hold on the *critical* imagination, but Lewis's apparently more naïve *Lion, Witch and Wardrobe* has a considerably vaster audience and continuing cultural appeal. There is a serious issue at stake in the vertiginous contrast between these narrative works and the ideas they capture for posterity.

Bataillean fantastic narrative is considered critically valuable because it participates in the transgression of distinctions between coherence and incoherence. Rosemary Jackson celebrates this kind of 'Fantastic' representation as a 'self-conscious confrontation of human-ism with something *on the edge*, something beyond, or before, or outside human culture'.[197] The alternative mode of 'Fantastic' narrative available from the very 'English' tradition represented by Lewis (and extended in the work of his Catholic friend JRR Tolkien) is rejected in the same breath for advocating 'a lesser version of religious myths, re-working the redemptive story of Christ's death and resurrection'.[198] The extraordinarily *popular* narrative fantasies pro-duced by the 'Inklings' is not proper 'Fantasy', then, (challenging the humanistic impulses of orderly literature) because it is already situated 'outside the human':

> An imagined realm with its own order, it is free from the demands of historical time, or of morality. Tolkien sees the function of faery as three-fold: to provide recovery, escape and consolation; it promises wish-fulfilment, magical satisfaction.[199]

This more popular literary fantasy makes the reader 'passive' by discouraging 'belief in the importance or effectiveness of action'. Not only does such consolatory fiction *do* nothing, it engenders inactivity in the reader:

> for their narratives are 'closed' ... [t]heir utopianism does not directly engage with divisions or contradictions of subjects *inside* human culture: their harmony is established on a mystical cosmic level.

Mystical, cosmic harmony – outside of human history or range of agency – is 'conservative' harmony, performing 'social and instinctual repression'.[200]

Similar arguments hover in the air concerning Jane Austen's 'conservative' narrative fictions, which offer imaginative consolation for the material conditions that delimit and distort women's lives in the idealized realm of the 'happy ending'. Or, at best, she allows for a critique of this very fictional fantasy by revealing its structure through irony. But a trip to any second-hand bookshop, charity shop, jumble sale will in most cases find several editions of the literary fantasies of Austen, Lewis and Tolkien; well-thumbed, much-loved, enjoyed and entirely understood beyond the icy grasp of professional criticism. Tom Shippey notes with some wonder that popular literary polls between 1997–2005 unfailingly made *Lord of the Rings* the 'best' or 'most popular' book in the 20th-century English literary tradition (apart from in Wales, where in the 1996 Waterstone's survey and Channel Four's 'Book Choice', the majority voted for *Ulysses* . . .)[201] This pattern was repeated in 2005 when the BBC's 'Big Read' poll placed Tolkien first and Austen's *Pride and Prejudice* second.[202] When I raised this phenomenon with a practising novelist recently he remarked that the kind of people who take part in these polls 'don't read much'. How much is enough? And why do people who are at least trying to find out about themselves and the world through reading, if they are not directed by professional criticism, invariably end up reading Austen, Lewis and Tolkien?

Whatever the critical arguments, Lewis and Tolkien have an extraordinary hold on the imagination of the vulgar populace: particularly among children and the under-educated. Shippey understands the strong tendency in intellectual appraisal to reject Tolkien's vast impact on the popular reading public as symptomatic of a deeper and less conscious rejection of 'the vulgar' itself:

> It did not provide that comfortable sense of superiority to the masses without which the English-speaking literary intellectual, it seems, cannot cope at all.[203]

That excessively popular and enduring love for the Inklings' mode of 'Fantasy' still tends to be charged as '. . . a kind of literary disease, whose sufferers – the millions of readers of fantasy – should be scorned, pitied, or rehabilitated back to correct and proper taste'.[204]

Fortunately for my nerve in making this argument, I never suffered hobbit fever in my formative years. It simply passed me by, the boyish domain of my older brother. Until, that is, the release of Jackson's extraordinary film adaptations of the new Millenium. These films crept up and over me before I had time to gather my critical wits in defence. And then I remembered that the first book which really made me cry, alone in my bedroom without witness, was Lewis's *The Last Battle*. Tolkien and Lewis have long been side-lined as neo-Victorian patricians lost to the progressive critical tradition since Leavis's turn from the philological methodology. It may be impossible now to understand Lewis as anything other than a patrician neo-Victorian conservative, thankfully irrelevant to the questions surging through the Humanities today. The Inklings, however, for all their discomforting 'Englishness' also produced, as Shippey notes, literature and criticism that offers a 'deeply serious response to what will be seen in the end as the major issues of [the] century: the origin and nature of evil'.[205]

Almost a year ago now, I found . . . an enchanted ray of sun. Just barely piercing the November mist, through rotten vegetation and magical ruins, this ray of sun illuminated before me an old pane of glass in the window of an abandoned house . . . I had just crossed through a forest after having abandoned Laure's coffin to the gravediggers. I saw this pane of glass, covered in almost a century of dust, from outside . . . If some vision of rot and decay had appeared to me in this abandoned place given over to the slow ravages of death, I would have looked at it like a faithful image of my own sorrow. I waited, I waited endlessly for the world of my desolation to open before me. I waited and I trembled. What I saw through the window to which aberration had led me was, on the contrary, the image of life and its most cheerful vagaries. Within my reach, behind the pane, was a brightly-colored collection of exotic birds. I could not have imagined anything sweeter beneath the dust, behind the dead branches and crumbling stone than these silent birds left behind by the departed master of this house.[206] [Bataille]

It is not difficult to argue that Lewis's work offers as close an engagement with the problem of evil as Bataille's. My purpose in raising this contrast is to suggest that a head-long rush into 'Transgression' is not the only available response to the moral melt-down of the 20th century. English critical thought, in response to the totalitarian disasters radiating across Europe in the first half of the century – echoes of which continue to terrorize the dream of universal progress – articulated a quietly contrasting mode of imaginative resistance. The continental figure of transgression crystallized into consciousness by Bataille has long-since fitted itself to the critical space vacated by the tidal regression of the Marxian critical paradigms that once dominated consciously *radical* or *transformative* criticism. The alternative paradigm for critical thought available through the pre-post-modern English critical tradition represented by Lewis has now been largely dismissed as irrelevant to the project of critical thought itself. This dismissal witnesses a broad acceptance of the higher virtues of transgression.

Bataille's life has been documented in fascinating detail by Surya's 'intellectual' biography, from which I have drawn insights throughout this discussion. The personal is critical: Bataille's life and work mirror each other in mutually informing ways. Lewis's later life has been well-documented in the bio-pic *Shadowlands*, a narrative centred on his strange and beautiful encounter with Joy Davidson; the married, American, ex-Communist poet who became his wife in 1957. That story is of interest in itself. Joy had written to Lewis from the States in response to admiring his work and they began an ongoing correspondence from 1950. She came to visit with her two young sons and soon revealed that her marriage was failing. Following her divorce, Lewis agreed to marry to allow her to remain in the UK with her sons. When she was found to be dying shortly afterwards he owned the marriage publicly and moved Joy and her boys into 'the Kilns', the house he had shared for many years with his older brother Warnie. Joy famously went into a staggering remission and lived a relatively normal married life with Lewis until her death in 1960:

> I have stood by the bedside of a woman whose thigh-bone was eaten through with cancer and who had thriving colonies of the disease in many other bones as well. It took three people to move her in bed. The doctors predicted a few months of life: the nurses (who often knew better) a few weeks. A good man laid his hands on her and prayed. A year later the patient was walking (uphill too, through rough woodland) and the man who took the last X-ray photographs was saying 'These bones are as solid as rock.' It's miraculous.[207]

She was dead the following year. The film captures the arc of this extraordinary story, but inevitably cuts some of the more challenging detail. One of the sons, absent from the film, was considerably disturbed by his parents' divorce. More significantly, Lewis was not the sweet old bachelor who had always lived alone with his brother, Warnie, and followed the same bed-time ritual each night before his life was transformed by Joy. Lewis had bought and shared his house ('the Kilns') with another, older married women until her death in 1951.

Mrs Moore, fondly known as 'Minto', was the mother of a friend of Lewis who had died in the first war, since which time he had taken it upon himself to look after her. The relationship never seems to have been discussed openly with anyone else, and there are no writings to give us a glimpse apart from Warnie's increasingly exasperated diaries:

> Six years before her actual death she thought she was dying, she went to the kitchen in The Kilns, and shovelled all Jack's early letters to her into the stove. When he first knew her, even when he was going to visit her in the afternoons, he had written to her every day. There was a lot to destroy.[208]

A. N. Wilson seems convinced that the relationship testifies to Lewis's early sado-masochistic interests. This is one way to account for a long-term, intensely private relationship between the precocious scholar and a bossy, uneducated woman some twenty years his senior which dominated Lewis's life from 1918:

> There are some men who pay prostitutes not for overtly sexual favours, but for humiliation of the most humdrum kind. Such people, caught in a strange web of masochism, find their emotional fulfilment not in acts of love but in being made to scrub kitchen floors or scour out pans. 'He was as good as an extra maid,' said Minto.[209]

Warnie, who called his brother Jack, described the relationship with Minto as 'the rape of J's life'.[210] Lewis never described it directly, but he might come closest to illuminating it in the description of 'courtly' convention given in *Allegory of Love*:

> To leap up on errands, to go through hot or cold, at the bidding of one's lady, or even of any lady, would seem but honourable and natural to gentleman of the thirteenth or even of the seventeenth century; and most of us have gone shopping in the twentieth with ladies who showed no sign of regarding the tradition as a dead letter.[211]

Lewis's strongest encounters with women ended in death. His mother's illness and death when he was a child is described with brief power in *Surpised by Joy*:

> There came a night when I was ill and crying both with headache and toothache and was distressed because my mother did not come to me.[212]

'Minto' died after an exhaustingly (especially for Lewis) long illness, during which he wrote *The Lion, the Witch and the Wardrobe*.

Lewis was a key figure in the Oxford English faculty. He participated in the construction of English as a professional discipline, alongside his fellow Inkling J.R.R. Tolkien, who also contributed to the history of the language (he drafted significant chunks of the first edition of the *OED*). These were unashamed traditionalists and 'elitists'. How did it happen, then, that their narrative works quickly became, and have long remained, beloved objects of the popular imagination? Why is their writing not spurned by those it would arguably oppress? I can't believe that Bataille, writing on the side of infernal liberation, is *really* read by anyone but radical academic theorists. If he *is* read by anyone for reasons other than studying intellectual history I would rather not be introduced to them.

Lewis's famous wardrobe provides a concrete figure for his imaginative resistance: a common-place domestic object which doubles as a portal into an alternative truth. The wardrobe made famous by Lewis's fable functions as the impossible threshold to a world of unlimited creative possibility; the wardrobe provides the narrative means to encounter mythic reality:

> And shortly after that they looked into a room, that was quite empty except for one big wardrobe; the sort that has a looking-glass in the door. There was nothing else in the room at all except a dead bluebottle on the window-sill . . . There was nothing Lucy liked so much as the smell and feel of fur. She immediately stepped into the wardrobe and got in among the coats and rubbed her face against them, leaving the door open, of course, because she knew that it is very foolish to shut oneself into any wardrobe.[213]

Bataille had also imagined a 'large antique bridal wardrobe' in *Story of the Eye* (as well as that 'fly', whose parallel in Lewis's tale lies dead on the windowsill). However, Bataille's wardrobe is there for Marcelle to shut herself inside ('very foolish') and masturbate miserably during the first orgy of *Story of the Eye*. When she sees the wardrobe again later in the narrative, she remembers the scene of horror and kills herself.

Lewis's wardrobe opens onto somewhere entirely unexpected; an imagined time and space inspiring hope, forgiveness and virtuous heroism. Bataille's wardrobe is self-enclosed, leading back to where it was entered. It offers an uncomfortable space for isolated, traumatized masturbation and frenzied hallucination. It opens again only to reveal the degraded scene of broken glass, blood and vomit that follow from the 'brutal onslaught of cunts and cocks' that sent Marcelle to take refuge in there in the first place.[214]

> Half an hour later, when I was less drunk, it dawned on me that I ought to let Marcelle out of her wardrobe: the unhappy girl, naked now, was in a dreadful state. She was trembling and shivering feverishly. Upon seeing me she displayed a sickly but violent terror.[215]

She is never quite the same again.

Lewis enjoyed a naïve and largely forgotten sense of what literature might be *for*. Only the 'vulgar' still get this point, because only the 'vulgar' (the largely uneducated masses who still exist, those millions who have perhaps read Tolkien, Austen and little else of any note, epitomized by the child reader of Lewis's *Narnia* cycle or the lay reader of Austen) are still superstitious enough to believe in evil and desire the good. What do I mean by 'the vulgar' here? The popular imagination, embodied in the under-educated, partially illiterate, feminine nonsense and childish fantasy; precisely that which is disciplined out of the intellectual mind and negated to produce the more cynical and advanced adamantine thought of the critically aware. Understood from this perspective the child-like taste for *Narnia* is also evidence of the persistence of a pre-enlightenment 'Imaginary' preserved in the minds and traditions of the culturally impoverished. This vulgar tradition is what is captured in popular forms of romance: the term now covers any form of fantasy that, in Germaine Greer's formulation, offers a shameful 'flight from reality'.[216] That 'flight' is mediated through the figure of the narrative possibility of a 'happy ending', where no such ending exists anywhere to be found in reality.

That 'flight from reality' is arguably the field of literature. The act of engaging in a work of fiction immediately turns the mind from the material to the ideational; from the real to the imaginary. What happens in the imaginary realm is then *always* imaginary: it either conforms to the shape of the 'real' as experienced outside the act of reading or it doesn't. It simply isn't the case that some literary fantasy is more 'real' than others. Some conforms more closely to the contours of the material world in which the fantasy took shape, others displace the action of the world into a clearer space for closer inspection, or invert the order of things and reveal order by its inversion. Literature is always of the mind.

Lewis was aware of critical tendencies to associate the baser forms of experience with 'reality' in contrast to the 'subjectivism' evidenced by experiences of beauty, or what Tolkien called 'sudden and miraculous grace'.[217] Lewis called it 'Joy'. The possibility of a beautified realism associated with myth has been reduced to the culturally degraded domain of the romantic and unreal, while 'reality' itself is recognizable by its ugliness:

> The materialist universe had one great, negative attraction to offer me. It had no other. And this had to be accepted; one had to look out on a meaningless dance of atoms (remember, I was reading Lucretius),

to realise that all the apparent beauty was a subjective phosphorescence, and to relegate everything one valued to the world of mirage.[218]

Lewis the 'idealist', on the other hand, did not reject vulgarity in his creative work, but associated the 'vulgar' itself with 'superiority':

> The unbeliever is always apt to make a kind of religion of his aesthetic experiences ... But the Christian knows from the outset that the salvation of a single soul is more important than the production or preservation of all the epics and tragedies in the world: and as for superiority, he knows that the vulgar since they include most of the poor probably include most of his superiors. He has no objection to comedies that merely amuse and tales that merely refresh ...[219]

He articulated the alternative (more sophisticated) position, which we recognize as transgression, through his eloquent demon *Screwtape*:

> We are really faced with a cruel dilemma. When the humans disbelieve in our existence we lose all the pleasing results of direct terrorism and we make no magicians. On the other hand, when they believe in us, we can't make them materialists and sceptics. At least, not yet. I have great hopes that we shall learn in due time how to emotionalise and mythologise their science to such an extent that what is, in effect, a belief in us (though not under that name) will creep in while the human mind remains closed to belief in the Enemy [God].

He lists the potential for human belief in 'Life Force', 'the worship of sex', and 'some aspects of Psychoanalysis' as 'useful' in achieving the demon's 'perfect work':

> the Materialist Magician, the man, not using, but veritably worshipping, what he vaguely calls 'Forces' while denying the existence of 'spirits' ...[220]

Tolkien in particular never denied that his own narrative work was, indeed, 'escapist' but instead put a very serious gloss on 'Escape':

> In what the misusers of Escape are fond of calling Real Life, Escape is evidently as a rule very practical, and may even be heroic. In real life it is difficult to blame it, unless it fails; in criticism it would seem to be the worse the better it succeeds. ... Why should a man be scorned, if, in finding himself in prison, he tries to get out and go home? Or if, when he cannot do so, he thinks and talks about other topics than jailers and prison-walls?[221]

Lewis and Bataille both had experiences from which to 'escape'; living and serving as they did through the two European wars, the second of which crystallized the eternal concern of the 'problem of evil' in a startlingly concrete and peculiarly modern way. Rosemary Jackson's critical sneer at the 'Oxford professor of philology' suggests that their professional status might alone be enough to condemn the Inklings' literary fantasies to the world of decadent privilege divorced from the material concerns of the modern world. Is philology a moral issue?

The Inklings are charged, then, with participating in a 'romance tradition supporting a ruling ideology . . . nostalgic for a pre-Industrial, indeed a pre-Norman Conquest, feudal order.' Again this perceived conservatism aligns them with Austen's rural English nostalgia. Austen also wrote in the face of 'progress' in the form of the first serious wave of industrialization. This kind of work does, as Jackson notes, establish 'a naïve equation of industry with evil'. The disgust expressed by Tolkienian fantasy for the 'materialism of a Robot Age' looks back with romantic longing to 'a medieval paradise' which 'allies morality and aesthetics': virtue is beautiful as the Elves, evil is ugly as the Orcs. The romance fantasy for Jackson is regressive; it implies that the 'only way is backwards:'

> C.S. Lewis's *Perelandra* trilogy, his Christian parable, *The Lion, the Witch and the Wardrobe* . . . are all of the same kind, functioning as conservative vehicles for social and instinctual repression.[222]

Well, the physical and material can be pretty repulsive when you think about it, especially when you have witnessed the slaughter of your generation in a war that expressed just such robotic materialism at work, and then lived through a second that distilled the ugliness of evil on an unprecedented scale. Some forms of 'social and instinctual repression' might be encouraged. We are now in a position to reflect on the Western narrative of industrial 'progress' differently. Romance fantasies offer an alternative narrative which preserves the imaginative possibility of a happy ending.

Jackson is only looking for a more *transgressive* fantasy: one that would expose the façade of ideology by which the contemporary world functions to oppress the very 'masses' who cling to their fantasies, and by doing so to release primordial drives towards a repressed revolutionary impulse. This has become a hegemonic critical stance. She wants a 'subversive' fantasy that touches the bonds of oppression and releases by its touch:

> Whereas more subversive texts activate a dialogue with this death drive, directing their energy towards a dissolution of repressive structures,

these more conservative fantasies simply go along with a desire to cease 'to be', longing to transcend or escape the human.[223]

Some aspects of 'the human' might need to be escaped; not everything 'human' is worth conserving, in fact much of it demands outright repression. Moreover, it is still not entirely clear to me yet what 'the human' denotes, given the extraordinary range of actions available to a modern human individual in the relative economic and moral freedom enjoyed by contemporary Western citizens. As I started to write this, in the week before Christmas, five young prostitute's bodies were gently decaying following the inexplicable violence of a single 'human'. As I now come back to revise it, a young boy has died in his mother's arms after being shot on his way home from football practice. These are only the most ridiculously local examples that come to mind. I don't have the strength to look any further. The 'problem of evil' is unanswered and unanswerable by the technological achievements of the post-industrial age. Jackson has argued strongly that the intended mythopoesis of Tolkien and Lewis is naïve, repressive and ahistorical. Let's put this now familiar claim to the test before we continue to search for an ever-more transgressive literature, criticism, or way of life.

Tolkien and Lewis were consciously engaged with generating and preserving what we might call 'mythic consciousness'. It is because 'mythic consciousness' operates outside of history that their work is now considered shamefully *ahistorical*. The ahistorical has become a critical sin. The *philological* approach to history that underpins the Inklings' imaginative work, or the *romantic* approach to history that characterizes Austen's narrative work, foreground a methodology now largely expunged from the contemporary academy:

> Philology has been dethroned from the high place it once had in this court of inquiry . . . Mythology is not a disease at all, though it may like all human things become diseased. You might as well say that thinking is a disease of the mind. It would be more near the truth today that languages, especially modern European languages, are a disease of mythology. But Language cannot, all the same, be dismissed. The incarnate mind, the tongue, and the tale are in our world coeval.[224]

The mythic itself has long been relegated to the place of pre-Enlightenment nonsense, superseded by more rational (largely scientific) epistemologies. Myth no longer organizes Western consciousness: except perhaps at Christmas, when it rises from the long-since to make us do things we would not normally consider doing, like dressing trees in the house, lighting the windows, feasting and economic purging. I can't help but wonder how Christmas is kept by Richard Dawkins.

Mythic consciousness persists, however, in the 'vulgar' forms of fairy-tale and romance. For Tolkien, fairy-tale is a mode of mythic narrative which remembers the possibility of a happy ending:

> Fairy-stories have in the modern lettered world been relegated to the 'nursery', as shabby or old-fashioned furniture is relegated to the play-room, primarily because the adults do not want it, and do not mind if it is misused. [*Note*: In the case of stories and other nursery lore, there is also another factor. Wealthier families employed women to look after their children, and the stories were provided by these nurses, who were sometimes in touch with rustic and traditional lore forgotten by their 'betters'. It is long since this source dried up, at any rate in England; but it once had some importance . . .][225]

Myth remains the cultural fodder of mothers and children, largely discarded in rational adulthood and the post-industrial culture in which 'rational adults' live. Luce Irigaray associates this 'problem' of mythic time with 'the entry of women into Western culture'. She has suggested that 'the problem is not to substitute one kind of temporality for another but to overcome this opposition and dichotomy'.[226] The opposition between myth and history is never clearly demarcated, seeming to be a matter of distance from the present:

> History often resembles 'Myth', because they are both ultimately of the same stuff. [Tolkien][227]

Bataille was openly engaged in a process of myth-making: '. . . the total world of myth, the world of *being*, is separated from the dissociated world by the very limits that separate the *sacred* from the *profane*'.[228] His various works aimed at the regeneration of a renewed mythic consciousness to overcome the Fascist appropriation of the modern world, otherwise resisted only by boredom:

> *Myth* remains at the disposal of one who cannot be satisfied by art, science, or politics. Even though love by itself constitutes a world, it leaves intact everything that surrounds it. The experience of love even augments lucidity and suffering; it develops the malaise and the exhausting impression of emptiness that results from contact with decomposed society. Myth alone returns, to the one who is broken by

every ordeal, the image of a plenitude extended to the community where men gather. Myth alone enters the bodies of those it binds and it expects from them the same receptiveness . . . For myth is . . . the divine figure of destiny and the world where this figure belongs and which ritually assumes its dominion.[229]

Myth operates for Bataille at the same level as erotic love, in that they both offer an experiential encounter with the sacred: 'Ritually lived myth reveals nothing less than true being.' In the 'sacred place' of myth (expressed at the most ordinary level by an experience of erotic love) 'human existence meets the figure of destiny' according to the 'caprice of *chance*' which is the 'opposite' to 'the *determining laws* that science defines':

myth enters into human existence like a force demanding that *inferior* reality submit to its dominion.

Anyone who has fallen in love will recognize something of this in the irresistible psychic tsunami which with bewildering suddenness reorders the immediate landscape.

Lewis was also concerned with this root fusion between erotic love and the sacred:

when at a later stage the explicitly sexual element awakes, he will soon feel (unless scientific theories are influencing him) that this had all along been the root of the whole matter . . . the incoming tide of Eros, having demolished many sand-castles and made islands of many rocks, has now at last with a triumphant seventh wave flooded this part of his nature also – the little pool of ordinary sexuality which was there on his beach before the tide came in. Eros enters him like an invader, taking over and reorganising, one by one, the institutions of a conquered country. It may have taken over many others before it reaches the sex in him; and it will reorganize that too.[230]

The final 'object of desire' of the quest obliquely narrated in the romantic myths of the Inklings is the same problem worked over incessantly and obsessively by Bataille. For Bataille as much as for Lewis and Tolkien, narrative literature provides a rare opportunity, alongside the experience of love and of death, to experience the sacred in a profane world:

In a sense, sacrifice was a novel, a fictional tale illustrated in a bloody manner . . . it is the narrative of a crime whose final episode is *performed* for the spectators by the priest and victim.[231]

The Lion, the Witch and the Wardrobe is famously centred on the sacrifice of Aslan: his dramatic loss to the children removes him as a source of direct comfort and living presence:

> At last she drew near. She stood by Aslan's head. Her face was working and twitching with passion, but his looked up at the sky, still quiet, neither angry nor afraid, but a little sad. Then, just before she gave the blow, she stooped down and said in a quivering voice, 'And now, who has won? Fool, did you think that by all this you would save the human traitor? Now I will kill you instead of him as our pact was and so the Deep Magic will be appeased. But when you are dead what will prevent me from killing him as well? And who will take him out of my hand *then*? Understand that you have given me Narnia for ever, you have lost your own life and you have not saved his. In that knowledge, despair and die.'[232]

Aslan's sacrifice quite simply offers a popular narrative encounter with the critical thought of the 'death of God'. Lewis achieved a concrete figure for the death of God, then, that had permeated the critical field at the time of writing his tale. He didn't rest with this thought but went further, to risk representing the idea of a subsequently strengthened renewal of divine power. He hints at his purpose here in *The Four Loves*:

> If we cannot 'practise the presence of God', it is something to practise the absence of God, to become increasingly aware of our unawareness till we feel like men who should stand beside a great cataract and hear no noise, or like a man in a story who looks in a mirror and finds no face there, or a man in a dream who stretches out his hand to visible objects and gets no sensation of touch. To know that one is dreaming is to be no longer perfectly asleep.[233]

Bataille and Lewis's generation faced the questions posed by the sacrifice of an old order, captured in this idea of the 'death of God'. Both answers are worthy of consideration today, as this remains a question faced anew by every living consciousness. We should be able to choose our own guides, and not have them chosen for us. Darko Suvin has recently problematized the idea of the 'death of God' in his survey of critical thought in the wake of socialism:

> The death of God should not mean the death of humanity. If God and Socialism are dead, it is not the case that everything is permitted (Dostoevsky, updated by Post-Modernist cynicism): it is rather the case that everything has to be rethought, and the rethinking then has to be tried out in practice.[234]

Transgression is one *part* of that process of rethinking, but certainly not the end of it.

Lewis's trademark Christianity was not the sort derided by A. C. Grayling. His late, painful and unwilled conversion is described in some detail in his brief autobiography, *Surprised by Joy*:

> The real terror was that if you seriously believed in even such a 'God' or 'Spirit' as I admitted, a wholly new situation developed. As the dry bones shook and came together in that dreadful valley of Ezekiel's, so now a philosophical theorem, cerebrally entertained, began to stir and heave and throw off its gravecloths, and stood upright and became a living presence. I was to be allowed to play at philosophy no longer... People who are naturally religious find difficulty in understanding the horror of such a revelation ... You must picture me alone in that room at Magdalen, night after night, feeling, whenever my mind lifted even for a second from my work, the steady, unrelenting approach of Him whom I so earnestly desired not to meet. That which I had greatly feared had at last come upon me. In the Trinity Term of 1929 I gave in, and admitted that God was God, and knelt and prayed: perhaps, that night, the most dejected and reluctant convert in all England. I did not see then what is now the most shining and obvious thing; the Divine humility which will accept a convert even on such terms. The Prodigal Son at least walked home on his feet. But who can duly adore that Love which will open the high gates to the prodigal who is brought in kicking, struggling, resentful, and darting his eyes in every direction for a chance of escape?[235]

Lewis's fall into undesired Christianity mirrors Bataille's fall into transgression. He sinks to his knees before the unavoidable presence of his living God in a scene that is reminiscent of a victim caught in one of de Sade's narratives, or of O's *liberation* by whips and chains:

> The hardness of God is kinder than the softness of men, and His compulsion is our liberation.[236]

A second key moment is also described in terms of a willing sacrifice:

> Without words and (I think) almost without images, a fact about myself was somehow presented to me. I became aware that I was holding something at bay, or shutting something out. Or, if you like, that I was wearing some stiff clothing, like corsets, or even a suit of armour, as if I were a lobster. I felt myself being, there and then, given a free choice. I could open the door or keep it shut; I could unbuckle the armour or keep it on. Neither choice was presented as a duty; no threat or promise was attached to either, though I knew that to open the door or take off the corset meant the incalculable. The choice appeared to be momentous but it was also strangely unemotional. I was moved by no desires or fears. In a sense I was not moved by anything. I chose to open, to unbuckle, to loosen the rein. I say, 'I chose,' yet it did not really seem possible to do the opposite.

The sacred enters Lewis's consciousness in scenes of unwilled seduction, a rape of his private self even:

> Eros enters him like an invader, taking over and reorganising, one by one, the institutions of a conquered country.[237]

He has been brought to knowledge of his living God precisely *against* his conscious will, in acknowledgement of a forceful 'necessity':

> Necessity may not be the opposite of freedom, and perhaps a man is most free when, instead of producing motives, he could only say, 'I am what I do.'[238]

Lewis's 'necessity' chimes with Bataille's vision of mythic 'chance' as the sign of a still-living sacred reality beyond the tedium of modern human life:

> Myth alone returns, to the one who is broken by every ordeal, the image of a plenitude extended to the community where men gather. Myth alone enters the bodies of those it binds and it expects from them the same receptiveness ... For myth is not only the divine figure of destiny and the world where this figure belongs and which ritually assumes its dominion ... myth enters into human existence like a force demanding that *inferior* reality submit to its dominion.[239]

Tolkien had also chosen the 'fairy tale' (or mythic narrative) as a mode of encountering the possibility of the sacred in a profane world:

> The consolation of fairy-stories, the joy of the happy ending: or more correctly of the good catastrophe, the sudden joyous 'turn' (for there is no true end to any fairy-tale): this joy, which is one of the things which fairy-stories can produce supremely well, is not essentially 'escapist', nor 'figurative'. In its fairy-tale – or otherworldly – setting, it is a sudden and miraculous grace: never to be counted on to recur. It does not deny the existence of *dycatastrophe*, of sorrow and failure: the possibility of these is necessary to the joy of deliverance; it denies (in the face of much evidence, if you will) universal final defeat and in so far is evangelium, giving a fleeting glimpse of Joy, Joy beyond the walls of the world, poignant as grief. It is the mark of a good fairy-story, of the higher or more complete kind, that however wild its events, however fantastic or terrible the adventures, it can give to child or man that hears it, when the 'turn' comes, a catch of the breath, a beat and lifting of the heart, near to (or indeed accompanied by) tears, as keen as that given by any form of literary art, and having a peculiar quality.[240]

This 'peculiar quality' of the mythic narrative is 'a sudden glimpse of the underlying reality or truth':

> It is not only a 'consolation' for the sorrow of this world, but a satisfaction, and an answer to that question, 'Is it true?' ... It is a serious and dangerous matter.[241]

I said that Lewis's conversion echoed Bataille's 'fall' into transgression. For Bataille there is a continuum of experience between the erotic and divine:

> I am by no means predisposed to think that voluptuous pleasure is the essential thing in this world. Man is more than a creature limited to its genitals. But they, those inavowable parts of him, teach him his secret.[242]

Lewis came to understand sex as a 'Pagan sacrament':

> In Friendship, as we noticed, each participant stands for precisely himself – the contingent individual that he is. But in the act of love we are not merely ourselves. We are also representatives. It is here no impoverishment but an enrichment to be aware that forces older and less personal than we work through us. In us all the masculinity and femininity of the world, all that is assailant and responsive, are momentarily focused. The man does play the Sky-Father and the woman the Earth-Mother; he does play Form, and she Matter. But we must give full value to the word *play* ... A woman who accepted as literally her own this extreme self-surrender would be an idolatress offering to a man what belongs only to God ... But within the rite or drama they become a god and goddess between whom there is no equality – whose relations are asymmetrical.[243]

When Lewis receives his experience of the sacred, then, he takes the symbolic role of the 'Earth-Mother' in 'self-surrender' to the super-masculinity of his God. This does sound a bit odd, but see how he represents final salvation as an 'invasion' by 'masculinity' to Jane, the female character central to *The Cosmic Trilogy* (1938–45):

> Some knowledge of a world beyond Nature she had already gained ... But she had been conceiving this world as 'spiritual' in the negative sense – as some neutral, or democratic, vacuum where differences disappeared, where sex and sense were not transcended but simply taken away. Now the suspicion dawned upon her that there might be differences and contrasts all the way up, richer, sharper, even fiercer, at every rung of the ascent. How if this invasion of her own being in marriage from which she had often recoiled, often in the very teeth of instinct, were not, as she had supposed, merely a relic of animal life or patriarchal barbarism, but rather the lowest, the first, and the easiest form of some shocking contact with reality which would have to be repeated – but in ever larger and more disturbing modes – on the highest levels of all?[244]

Her fears are explained as a naturally feminine aversion to an unavoidable masculinity in the face of which 'we are all feminine':

> You are offended by the masculine itself ... The male you could have escaped, for it exists only on the biological level. But the masculine none of us can escape. What is above and beyond all things is so masculine that we are all feminine in relation to it.[245]

The story that initiates Lewis's *Trilogy* in *Out of the Silent Planet* (1938) is that Ransome – the philologist hero modelled at least in part on Tolkien – has stumbled on a scheme of cosmic treachery. He is kidnapped while on a walking tour by a wayward rational scientist and his amoral financer on a trip to Mars (Malacandra) in a home-made space-ship. There he learns the Old Solar language from native inhabitants, lives among them, and discovers the final truth about the place of the Earth and human consciousness in a sacred cosmos. This is a narrative that claims ultimate importance and which is worth reading for its extraordinarily strange visions of alternative realities. Our hero travels in the second instalment willingly to Venus (Perelandra) where he encounters the goddess of Love and saves her from her fall; first through the delay of persistent rational argument, then finally through a prolonged bout of fisticuffs with the devil incarnate. He finally defeats the devil and is brought into the presence of the eldils (angels) and god-powers of the living universe. He returns in the final narrative, *That Hideous Strength*, as Mr King-Fisher. Now carrying a wound from his fight with the devil that will not heal, he revives Merlin from his long sleep, draws the new Logres around him, and saves a marriage on the way to saving the world from final engulfment in evil (Belbury). The narrative ends on a sanctified marriage-bed scene, in the copulating presence of elephants, bears, hedgehogs, mice and bats, as Perelandra's (as Venus) heavenly archetype descends to Earth:

> She comes nearer to the Earth than she was wont to – to make Earth sane. Perelandra is all about us and Man is no longer isolated. We are now as we ought to be – between the angels who are our elder brothers and the beasts who are our jesters, servants and playfellows.[246]

In sending Jane to her husband's bed the all-wise King-Fisher (Ransome) gives the final twist to the knife:

> Go in obedience and you will find love. You will have no more dreams. Have children instead.[247]

There is, as this particular narrative manifests, a latent eroticism about Christian love. Northrop Frye considered this point in some detail in his account of the Bible in Western literature:

> Anyone coming to the New testament from the outside may well wonder why we are presented in the Gospels with an incarnate god so hung up on sex that his followers claimed that his father was not his father and that his mother was a virgin.[248]

Frye was keen to remind us of the pivotal agency of female sexuality in the Christian meta-narrative:

> After Eve took the initiative in the Fall, the supremacy of the symbolically male is reflected in the supremacy of the sexually male in human society which God predicts will be the main result of the expulsion from the paradisal state. Theologians and commentators have been so anxious to emphasize this point that they have largely overlooked the central role of woman in the J account, and the fact that patriarchal societies are explicitly said to be the consequence of sin. Man falls as woman, that is, as sexual being, hence woman would have to be the central figure in the restoration of the original sexual and social state.[249]

For Frye, then, the Christian myth of fall and redemption *answers* the tragedy of that other 'universal' sexual myth, the Oedipus:

> The Oedipus quest is the tragic version of the Christian one ... The Oedipus who kills his father and possesses his mother sexually is the contrasting figure to the Christ who appeases the Father and rescues a bride who is symbolically very close to the mother.[250]

The Christian 'ascent [through sexuality] to love and beauty' has a 'demonic parody' in the mythopoesis of Western literature: 'the sado-masochistic cycle, in which the female may tyrannize over the male or vice-versa'. He adds, usefully, that 'the metaphorical link between nature and the female is usually preserved'. The fall into sadistic modes of pleasure characteristic of thought in the wake of the 'death of God' marks the final loss of what Luce Irigarary has called a possibility of 'horizontal transcendence':

> I think that to move beyond religious fundamentalism, a culture of two different subjects is necessary, that is a culture in which we have to coexist in difference and accept that our own values are not the sole and unique values. The worse conflicts happen between those who are the same and confront each other about their values, each one claiming to have reached the top ... Difference – of course not hierarchical, thus quantitative – is more able to pave the way towards peace. It could also allow us to avoid fundamentalisms, keeping the horizon of truth open, including religious truth. Difference, as I try to practise and promote, is also a means of each time respecting the otherness of the other, a thing that prepares for peace and coexistence with everyone.[251]

Bataille famously fell from a 'pious' form of Christianity into the syphilitic brothels of his imagination. His mature vision of GOD is a prostitute giving her wares freely and taking crazed and animalistic pleasure in the process. Lewis's pre-conversion sexuality took the form of a conscious sado-masochism:

> You must excuse (tho' I'm sure I don't care a damn if you don't, mon vieux!) this writing, as it's being done across my knee.
> 'Across my knee' of course makes one think of positions for Whipping: or rather not for whipping (you couldn't get any swing) but for that torture with brushes. This position, with its childish, nursery associations wd. have something beautifully intimate and also very humiliating for the victim.[252]

Lewis signed one letter of this sort 'Philomastix', which he later explained as 'a harmless piece of Greek affectation':

> 'philo' is the same word you see in 'philosopher' 'philologist' etc, and means 'fond of' while 'mastix' is the ordinary word for a whip.[253]

This co-mingling of Lewis's academic and sexual identities (a classical education is needed before one can conceive of oneself as 'Philomastix') led him to begin some research into his sexual tastes:

> I hope you are right as to the possibilities of my finding my particular kind of love. Butler tells me that the person to read on my subject is a Frenchman of the 17th century [sic] called the Visconte de Sade: his books, however, are very hard to come by.[254]

By 1930, Lewis is found reflecting on his youthful sexual fantasies. He foregrounds the interpenetration of his erotic and spiritual experiences:

> Indeed today – another of those days which I seem to have described so often lately, the same winter sunshine, the same gilt and grey skies shining thro bare shock-headed bushes, the same restful pale plough-land and grass, and more than usual of the birds darting out their sudden, almost cruelly poignant songs – to-day I got such a sudden intense feeling of delight that it sort of stopped me in my walk and spun me round. Indeed the sweetness was so great, & seemed so to affect the whole body as well as the mind, that it gave me pause – it was so very like sex.
> One knows what a psychoanalyst would say – it is sublimated lust, a kind of defeated masturbation which fancy gives one to compensate external chastity. Yet after all, why should that be the right way of looking at it? If he can say that *It* is sublimated sex, why is it not open to

> me to say that sex is undeveloped *It?* – as Plato would have said. And if
> as Plato thought, the material world is a copy or mirror of the spiritual,
> then the central feature of the material life (= sex), must be a copy of
> something in the Spirit: and when you get a faint glimpse of the latter, of
> course you find it like the former: an Original *is* like its copy: a man *is*
> like his portrait.[255]

His earlier letters refer to his s-m fantasies as 'It'.

The final phase of Lewis's cosmic narrative is set in Edgestow University English department, in which the academics fall prey to the fascinating figure of the louche financer of the first book, and his seductive ideas for capitalist innovations in the College. He offers access to a mysterious and successful financial venture that will guarantee future income and support research careers. A departmental meeting fails to recognize what is at stake in this new game, and ignores the cries of the old Professor who seems to stand against progress. The contract with the evil capitalist system leads to the deforestation of the ancient college grounds to make room for a shiny new international research institute. The research institute turns out to be the headquarters of the Belbury conspiracy, working to achieve a final modernity of pure evil. The woods, somewhat fortuitously, contain the undead body of Merlin, wizard of the Middle Ages, who is disturbed from his rest and returns to join spiritual forces with Fisher-King and his growing community of disciples. Only in the final scene, when the University and most of its inhabitants have been swallowed by a cosmic convulsion, does Lewis allow the allegory some self-consciousness:

> 'I know,' said Denniston. 'One's sorry for a man like Churchwood. I
> knew him well; he was an old dear. All his lectures were devoted to
> proving the impossibility of ethics, though in private life he'd walk ten
> miles rather than leave a penny debt unpaid. But all the same ... was
> there a single doctrine practised at Belbury which hadn't been preached
> by some lecturer at Edgestow? Oh, of course, they never thought anyone
> would *act* on their theories! No one was more astonished than they when
> what they'd been talking of for years suddenly took on reality. But it was
> their own child coming back to them: grown up unrecognizable, but
> their own'.[256]

Lewis's *Trilogy* turns out to be a crude but genuinely surprising narrative analysis of the forces manifesting in the Humanities through the concentrated lenses of European war (it was published between 1938 and 1945). It is a fantasy outlining the ethical and practical tendencies of the theories threatening at that point to take hold of the

European critical imagination: a prophecy of the rise of a philosophy of transgression in all but name:

> The physical sciences, good and innocent in themselves, had already, even in Ransome's own time, begun to be warped, had been subtly manoeuvred in a certain direction. Despair of objective truth had been increasingly insinuated into the scientists; indifference to it, and a concentration upon mere power, had been the result. ... Dreams of the far future destiny of man were dragging from its shallow and unquiet grave the old Man as God. The very experiences of the dissecting room and the pathological laboratory were breeding a conviction that the stifling of all deep-set repugnances was the first essential for progress. ... What should they find incredible, since they believed no longer in a rational universe? What should they regard as too obscene, since they held that all morality was a mere by-product of the physical and economic situations of men?[257]

Jane's husband, the young English lecturer drawn to Belbury by ambition, is given a straightforwardly theoretical analysis:

> It is incredible how little this knowledge moved him. It could not, because he had long ceased believing in knowledge itself. What had been in his far-off youth a merely aesthetic repugnance to realities that were crude or vulgar, had deepened and darkened, year after year, into a fixed refusal of everything that was in any degree other than himself. He had passed from Hegel into Hume, thence through Pragmatism, and thence through Logical Positivism, and out at last into the complete void. The indicative mood now corresponded to no thought that his mind could entertain. He had willed with his whole heart that there should be no reality and no truth, and now even the imminence of his own ruin could not wake him ... The last moments before damnation are not often so dramatic. Often the man knows with perfect clarity that some still possible action of his own will could save him. But he cannot make this knowledge real to himself. Some tiny habitual sensuality, some resentment too trivial to waste on a blue-bottle, the indulgence of some fatal lethargy, seems to him at that moment more important than the choice between total joy and total destruction. With wide eyes open, seeing that the endless terror is just about to begin and yet (for the moment) unable to feel terrified, he watches passively, not moving a finger for his own rescue, while the last links with joy and reason are severed, and drowsily sees the trap close upon his soul. So full of sleep are they at the time when they leave the right way.[258]

Jane's narrative is of the independent young woman learning that to achieve her liberation she must first submit to the rather terrifying reality of sexuality: a muted version of *Story of O*. Jane's marriage, after Perelandra's healing, finds itself in accord with the transgressive marriage of Bataille's *Eroticism*:

> This type of marriage is admittedly remote from the one we regard as truly human and humane, for we require freedom of choice on both sides. But neither does it lower women to the level of commerce and calculation. Women rank on a level with celebrations. A woman given in marriage has after all the same sort of significance as champagne has in our customs ... not primarily a symbol of social status but a natural stimulus.[259]

It's heady stuff indeed.

Thinking against transgression has dragged me through a powerful undercurrent of thought of the death of God. The thought remains with me. Recently, on a Sunday morning, as I came downstairs to make coffee before writing this, the TV was showing footage of the flooding of the south-east and midlands of the UK. Some media sofa-chat was going on concerning responsibility, government failure, insurance concerns. As I passed through the room to the kitchen an educated, white voice said clearly and in a tone of contempt: 'there are no acts of God *any more*'. I was struck by her untenable *confidence*.

Laure died in 1938. Bataille wrote 'a woman's death tore him apart'.[260] Joy died in 1960 following a brief period of unexpected and transformative intimacy with Lewis. Her death wrought an extended cry that became perhaps Lewis's most compelling work of non-fiction, *A Grief Observed* (1961):

> There are moments, most unexpectedly, when something inside me tries to assure me that I don't really mind so much, not so very much, after all. Love is not the whole of a man's life. I was happy before I ever met [Joy]. I've plenty of what are called 'resources'. People get over these things. Come, I shan't do so badly. One is ashamed to listen to this voice but it seems for a little to be making out good sense. Then comes a sudden jab of red-hot memory and all this 'commonsense' vanishes like an ant in the mouth of a furnace.[261]

This stream of grieving consciousness follows the swerve of Lewis's reflections, which pass inevitably from the death of his wife to the death of his God:

> Come, what do we gain by evasions? We are under the harrow and can't escape. Reality, looked at steadily, is unbearable. And how or why did such a reality blossom (or fester) here and there into the terrible phenomenon called consciousness? Why did it produce things like us who can see it and, seeing it, recoil in loathing?[262]

Facing the logical inevitability of atheist materialism once his belief in a loving God had been threatened with the extreme pain his wife suffered and by which she was finally destroyed, Lewis simply recoiled. He diverted the resulting stream of thought into projection of a 'Cosmic Sadist' or 'spiteful imbecile' in place of the loving God of Christian myth:

> Kind people have said to me 'She is with God.' In one sense that is most certain. She is, like God, incomprehensible and unimaginable.[263]

His response to the actual (rather than theoretical) and full (rather than partial) 'dissolution' that comes with grief following death of the love object leads him to the question on which the critical thought of transgression has turned:

> I am more afraid that we are really rats in a trap. Or, worse still, rats in a laboratory. Someone said, I believe, 'God always geometrizes'. Supposing the truth were 'God always vivisects?[264]

Rather than accept the 'death of God' that would offer the ground for transgression, however, Lewis elaborated an alternative path from stunned, snarling grief towards a new sense of his living God:

> Bridge-players tell me there must be some money on the game 'or else people won't take it seriously'. Apparently it's like that. Your bid – for God or no God, for a good God or the Cosmic Sadist, for eternal life or non-entity – will not be serious if nothing much is staked on it. .. The terrible thing is that a perfectly good God is in this matter hardly less formidable than a Cosmic Sadist. The more we believe that God hurts only to heal, the less we can believe that there is any use in begging for tenderness. A cruel man might be bribed – might grow tired of his vile sport – might have a temporary fit of mercy, as alcoholics have fits of sobriety. But suppose that what you are up against is a surgeon whose intentions are wholly good. The kinder and more conscientious he is, the more inexorably he will go on cutting. If he yielded to your entreaties, if he stopped before the operation was complete, all the pain up until that point would have been useless. But is it credible that such extremities of torture should be necessary for us? Well, take your choice. The tortures occur. If they are unnecessary, then there is no God or a bad one. If there is a good God, then those tortures are necessary ... Either way we are for it.[265]

Gods, like the people they represent, must needs die. We should remain conscious that they also have a tendency – like Dr Who – to regenerate as and when you least expect it: 'A God who was more than can be expressed, who exceeds all categories of definition and control is a Queer God indeed.'[266] Such a God would not tolerate repression or regression.

The thought of the continuing relevance of a 'platitudinous, universal moral law', apprehended in the light of a sublimated rather than repressed sexuality is not necessarily a step back into pre-Enlightenment superstition:

> We have only two alternatives. Either the maxims of traditional morality must be accepted as axioms of practical reason and neither admit nor require argument to support them and not to 'see' which is to have lost human status; or else there are no values at all, what we mistook for values being 'projections' of irrational emotions. It is perfectly futile, after having dismissed traditional morality with the question, 'Why should we obey it?' then to attempt the reintroduction of value at some later stage in our philosophy. Any value we reintroduce can be countered in just the same way. Every argument used to support it will be an attempt to derive from premises in the indicative mood to a conclusion in the imperative. And this is impossible.[267]

Critical thought of transgression is close to deriving an unjustifiable 'imperative' from an understandable 'indicative'.[268]

All are writing for truth and freedom, but for Lewis '[t]he very idea of freedom presupposes some objective moral law which overarches rulers and ruled alike'. For Lewis the acknowledgement of a 'platitudinous, universal moral law' was simply the ground condition for the possibility of a true democracy:

> Unless we return to the crude and nursery-like belief in objective values, we perish. If we do, we may live, and such a return might have one minor advantage. If we believed in the absolute reality of elementary moral platitudes, we should value those who solicit our votes by other standards than have recently been in fashion. While we believe that good is something to be invented, we demand of our rulers such qualities as 'vision', 'dynamism', 'creativity', and the like. If we returned to the objective view we should demand qualities much rarer, and much more beneficial – virtue, knowledge, diligence and skill. 'Vision' is for sale, or claims to be for sale, everywhere. But give me a man who will do a day's work for a day's pay, who will refuse bribes, who will not make up his facts, and who has learned his job.[269]

Criticism has long been seduced by transgression, it might be time to shake ourselves out of this particular intoxication and consider the virtues still available to critical thought. *Against Transgression* has been an attempt to engender a possibility of thought that concerns the immediate present, rather than a longing for a mythic past or unobtainable promise of future bliss. Transgression asked us to breach our boundaries in the name of liberation: compassion would answer that there is still a point in desiring virtue. There are as many ways to experience continuity as there are discontinuous subjects, and it is worth experimenting with as many as possible before falling in with Bataille. Like learning to swim with the tide rather than waving and drowning.

Lewis was evidently aware of the emergence of a 'Nietschzean ethic' in his lifetime:

> the Nietzschean ethic can be accepted only if we are ready to scrap traditional morals as a mere error and then put ourselves in a position where we can find no ground for any value judgments at all. It is the difference between a man who says to us: 'You like your vegetables moderately fresh, why not grow your own and have them perfectly fresh?' and a man who says, 'Throw away that loaf and try eating bricks and centipedes instead.' Real moral advances, in fine, are made *from within* the existing moral tradition and can be understood only in the light of that tradition. The outsider who has rejected the tradition cannot judge them. He has, as Aristotle said, no *arche*, no premises.[270]

Lewis and Bataille found a powerful truth in their relative encounters with Nietszche's writings. Lewis's response has now largely been expunged from the literary and critical tradition. He is not mentioned in the most recent Routledge or Oxford *History of English Literature*, but his work cumulatively begs a question that remains largely unanswerable by the terms of today's academy:

> Were the old myths truer than the new myths?[271]

The newer myth of transgressive (sexual) 'liberation' has been written across the older myth of an arguably *more* radical dream of 'salvation'.

Transgression is a concept tied up with human desire and its constraints. It is situated within a Christian (typically Catholic) paradigm of sin and atonement. What is intriguing is that it does so in unselfconscious disavowel of the spiritual and moral tradition from which these ideas have emerged, and seems to have repressed the second half of that otherwise promising story. Colette Peignot noticed this inverted Catholicism as the prime mover of Bataille's life and work:

> And you pretend to be inspired by Sade! . . . You are in fact inspired by Catholic priests. Instead of libertinism which could be a sort of powerful and happy impulse *even without Crime* you want bitterness *between* us. You look like a child coming out of the confessional, sure to return.
> Like a priest with nasty habits.[272]

Transgression asks us to reconsider human agency and responsibility following the thought of the 'death of God'. Nick Land has recently argued that '[t]he death of God is the ultimate transgression, the release of humanity from itself, back into the blind infernal extravagance of the sun.'[273] If it were the 'ultimate transgression', there would be nothing left to transgress. Lewis's inverse movement, his turn *to* a living Christian 'God' nonetheless, was an equally breathtaking act of opening out the self to something radically unknown. This is also a transgression of the terms of 'ordinary' human-ness. In an intriguing way it follows a parallel movement to O's realization of feminine 'emptiness', as well as to Bataille's submission to mythic chance. From this perspective Lewis's cry for a 'universal morality', as a boundary curtailing the otherwise extra-ordinary range of human action, tightens the cords against which transgression enjoys struggling. Morality is after all still necessary for transgression: the 'chokehold that makes you come'. Lewis did in the end find his 'particular kind of love'. His fall into Christianity turned out to have been the best s-m of all.

4

Preface to Compassion

Our assertions turn against us. Everything defeats the purpose. Thought hinders gesture, and we stand there, stuck. Thought? No: facts, history, men and their backward language. So these ideas are shaken up as in a game of jacks? But one cannot save oneself on paper like a drowning person clings to a rock: the sheet is smooth, smooth, smooth and good will slips through your fingers like an eel. Paper is milksop, dried paste with words worn thin. Adhesion, abdication, this is easy to say. But all this is life without your being able to get out of it. Go on, then, see thought through to the end, see it through in all its consequences. But you speak in a low voice as in a house of the dead... Perhaps the moment will come when it will be enough to know what one is against.[274] (Laure)

A woman who rejects her mother, such as Madame de Saint-Ange, such as Eugénie, finds herself in an unbearable position. In the patriarchal society, for women freedom is untenable.[275] (Acker)

Now do not put a ribbon in your hair;
Abjure the spangled insult of design,
The filigree sterility, nor twine
A flower with your strength; go bare, go bare.[276] (Joy)

This was always going to be a tricky discussion to conclude, so I am going to avoid conclusion altogether and offer a short preface to compassion instead. All I really wanted to say was that I am sick of transgression. The world seems sick of transgression also; sick and dying. There has to be more to us than the Sisyphus-like compulsion to create order in order to enjoy kicking it over. Sandcastles again. Or if there isn't at least I have decided to rest for a while in the illusion that there is. This is a kind of intellectual freedom.

I honestly didn't expect transgression to lead back to God, but there it goes, twisted in hideous contortions of anguish at the thought of the intellectual crime of the second Millenium. This is the third Millenium. We have time to take a breath and start fresh. Or do we?

> As we may learn from such disparate sources as the *Oresteia* and *Psycho*, matricide is of all possible individual crimes the most insupportable psychologically. And, of all possible crimes which an entire culture can commit, the one most difficult to bear, psychologically, is deicide.[277] [Sontag]

Luce Irigaray has invited us to believe that 'culture' as such is founded on symbolic matricide. Without matricide we could not enjoy culture. Without symbolic matricide I wouldn't be able to write at all. The mother has to be killed off to allow the dream of language. Maybe matricide and deicide are not that far apart after all.

Kathy Acker is one of the best readers of Irigaray, as well as of de Sade and Bataille. Acker was a beautifully transgressive woman. She more than most had 'mastered' the art of transgression in life and in writing. Her writing is almost unreadable as a result, but something fascinating and possibly unrepeated glistens in its labyrinthine counter-structures. One of the last things Kathy Acker wrote was a piece for *Critical Quarterly* (1995) called 'Seeing Gender'. I don't think she knew she was dying when she wrote it, but she died two years later following a double mastectomy for which she paid $4000 of the money she gleaned from her unreadable writing. Maybe some of this money came from publishing in *CQ*. I like to think so. She begins:

> When I was a child, the only thing I wanted was to be a pirate.[278]

She might have written well on *Pirates of the Caribbean*. She would have enjoyed that searing line in the third film of the series: 'the immaterial is now immaterial'. It's spoken by the East India Company, but you have to listen hard to catch it. The immaterial became immaterial at the end of the 18th century. Only the material survives industrialization. Pirates, or privateers, negotiated the dangerous back waters of early capitalism. We still love them because they alone ran circles for a while around the rampant materialism of the East India Company and its economic globalism. Pirates embody freedom from economic determinism. Even Disney knows this. Female pirates were few and far between, but they existed. I understand that two of them ended up on the same ship and fell in love, missing that fact that they were both disguised as pirate men. Kathy Acker was a fine literary pirate. She pillaged the best of them.

I'd like to end with the otherwise unrelated voices of this assemblage of remarkable literary women: Kathy Acker, who did become a pirate; Colette Peignot, who was the only really *literate* woman to fuck Bataille (without having to be paid to do so) and wrote well of it; Joy Davidman, the ex-Communist poet who fell for Lewis through his dream of Narnia and stopped writing in order to concentrate on love and dying; and Susan Sontag, who understood all of this much better than I think I can but still died nonetheless. Compassion comes last of all.

Kathy Acker is one of few who understood Bataille's experiment with an Acéphalic society:

> Another form of Acéphale – there is no one *authoritative* image – is also headless; this time the head is a skull at the place of, in the place of, the genitalia. Here is the place where the logos ought to be or is. In personal language, the head is ruled by the cunt.
>
> Moreover, the head is a skull. It is said that in the Middle Ages, monks contemplated skulls in order to see God or Truth. To see clearly is to perceive that one must die. The logos must realize that it is part of the body and that this body is limited. Subject, not to the mind, but to death. Here is the place of sex.[279]

Acker was 'looking' for her body when she died, and claimed she had found 'all the answers' to a lifetime of questions. She wrote of the 'other' body she had experienced in writing:

> When the colon or the labyrinth is center, our center, we, human, learn how little, if anything, we know and can know. Since the law presupposes knowledge, we learn to distrust the law.
>
> A colon's end is shit. Not transcendence, but waste. Beyond meaning. For the head is no longer the head; we live, perceive, and speak, in our bodies and through our bodies. There is no escape from that, us, which is subject to death and will become excrement – this is the Nietzschean 'Eternal Return' – there is no escape from this labyrinth.[280]

She read Bataille, in the way she read de Sade, as a 'male' writer writing in full knowledge and immanent critique of patriarchy. It is possible that I have mis-read them, these transgressive men, too ready to take offence and overlooking the point that they also wanted my freedom (at least theoretically):

I, Ariadne, enabled my lover to kill the monster in the center of the labyrinth and to escape that labyrinth. I, Ariadne, defeated the labyrinth made by the artist, Daedalus.

For the sake of love.

Then my lover abandoned me. Because he found someone else. Or because Dionysus, more powerful than my lover, wanted me, fucked me, then slew me.

I did not escape love's labyrinth.

This is the dream. The dream of the labyrinth or the self that will lead us to languages that cannot be authoritarian.[281]

Kathy Acker, in looking for her body, was looking for the possibility of a non-authoritarian language. A language of 'silences: secrets, autism, forgettings, disavowals, even death'. The language of silence 'so that we can hear the sounds of the body . . . the sounds of the unknown'.[282] For, according to the originary myth of the labyrinth, the 'first human artist was Daedalus. Was a male. Was, as artist, both inferior and subject to the representative of political power':

The labyrinth, that construction of Daedalus's, covered up the origin of art. Covered up the knowledge that art was, and so is, born out of rape or the denial of women and born out of political hegemony.

One form of Daedalus's construction is time. When time is understood as linear, there is no escape. No escape for us out of the labyrinth. I said that the labyrinth has been built.

But time is not only linear. Unlike Ariadne, for we do not hold Theseus as our lover, let us, by changing the linearity of time, deconstruct the labyrinth and see what the women who are in its center are doing. Let us see what is now central.[283]

I could go on quoting Acker for ever. A substitute for thought. As she says: 'In my confusion, I look to older writing, as I have often done when I am confused. I look to find a clue about my own writing.'[284] The clue is in the claim to a language of the body that is non-authoritarian. Acker quoting Butler: 'against those who would claim the body's irreducible materiality is a necessary condition for feminist practice, I suggest that prized materiality may well be constituted through an exclusion and a degradation of the feminine that is profoundly problematic for feminism.'[285]

For Bataille at his most atheistic, the disembodied language of reason is only a by-product of taboo. Tolkienian Catholicism comes uncannily close to Bataillean atheism on this point. Prohibition, taboo, moral rectitude, the freedom of restraint; all seem integral to and heightened by the experience of transgression. The 'maternal subject' is also a subject of transgression: she literally embodies (and remains conscious of) the 'fusion' of discontinuous subjects. If she's lucky she also experiences 'continuity' at conception. Had she not once been a subject of transgression, she would not retain this capacity to embody desire and prohibition for the infant. Mothers, as much as their children, are the product of transgression. For Susan Sontag, the problem at the centre of this labyrinthine discussion is concise:

> We live in a society whose entire way of life testifies to the thoroughness with which the deity has been dispatched, but philosophers, writers, men of conscience everywhere squirm under the burden. For it is a far simpler matter to plot and commit a crime than it is to live with it afterwards.[286]

One way to live with a crime is to encourage everyone else to repeat it so that it becomes common-place. Bataille set himself to reconcile 'what seems impossible to reconcile, respect for the law and violation of the law, the taboo and its transgression':[287]

> One thing or the other: either the taboo holds good, in which case the experience does not occur, or if it does, only furtively, outside the field of awareness; or it does not hold good; and of the two cases this is the more undesirable.[288]

We cannot rest in transgression. There is no rest in transgression.

> If we observe the taboo, if we submit to it, we are no longer conscious of it . . . in the act of violating it we feel the anguish of mind without which the taboo could not exist: that is the experience of sin.[289]

The experience of transgression is marked by this 'anguish of mind'. Susan Sontag identified contemporary 'Western' sensibility as embodied in the 'artist as exemplary sufferer':

> the sensibility we have inherited identifies spirituality and seriousness with turbulence, suffering, passion. For two thousand years, among Christians and Jews, it has been spiritually fashionable to be in pain.[290]

Sexuality is over-valued by our culture because it invites 'exquisite . . . suffering'.[291] The 'contemporary taste for the extreme in art and thought' for Sontag was evidence of the 'contradictory historical and intellectual experiences' of the era through which we are still living:

> Perhaps there are certain ages which do not need truth as much as they need a deepening of the sense of reality, a widening of the imagination.[292]

Under such conditions an 'idea which is a distortion may have greater intellectual thrust than the truth'. Transgression, an idea which is arguably a distortion, is not so much an index to the 'truth' as an index to the 'needs of the spirit' under such conditions. Rather than perpetuating and celebrating transgression, then, we might address the spiritual needs it articulates. It is possible to turn away from the anguish expressed by transgression without turning back.

Taking Simone Weil as her example, Sontag suggested that we 'read writers of such scathing originality for their personal authority, for the example of their seriousness, for their manifest willingness to sacrifice themselves for their truths' but not so much 'for their "views"':

> I cannot believe that more than a handful of the tens of thousands of readers she has won since the posthumous publication of her books and essays really share her ideas.[293]

Similarly, philosophy of the extreme anguish of mind is interesting for its extremity, but 'most of [Nietzsche's] modern admirers could not, and do not embrace [his] ideas.' It is difficult to embrace ideas which seem to *want* it to be the case that 'the promise of fulfilled immanence was available only to the few, the masters, and rested on a perpetuation or freezing of the historical impasse of a master-slave society'.[294] There is no rest in transgression.

Thinking against transgression, then, must entail having the courage to address Luce Irigaray's very difficult question:

> But whence comes the fact that suffering has so often been associated with form? Would this not be tied to the solitude of a man who claims, all alone, to construct and build the world? If form also results from the other, from the friendship that is felt toward the other and from the friendship that he, or she, offers, is its efflorescence not also happiness? Does the acceptance of a limit, of a not being the whole, necessarily imply grief? Or does it engender suffering only because of a mental pretension founded upon the forgetting of faithfulness to life, whose guarding and growth are accompanied by happiness, even if they require discipline and renunciation.[295]

The 'limit experience' of post-Foucaultian transgression limits the truth of subjectivity to the most *extreme* examples. Limits can be overrun, but they can also be the point of turning away. Turning away is nothing to be ashamed of, informed as we now are by the experience of the limit. Colette Peignot wrote to Bataille:

> Do not forget that I have some pretensions, too, and as much right as you to be inspired by Sade. I can still choose the role and interpret it as I wish ... – Your complete freedom and mine can be preserved more nobly, without even excluding the *burst of laughter*.[296]

Susan Sontag wrote that while 'all truth is superficial':

> Some (but not all) distortions of the truth, some (but not all) insanity, some (but not all) unhealthiness, some (but not all) denials of life are truth-giving, sanity-producing, health-creating, and life-enhancing.[297]

Kathy Acker claimed shortly before dying that she had 'beaten' the cancer. She had found her body in the experience of losing it.

And so we are left with a dilemma that can only really be described as *moral*. The sexual revolution *did* happen, albeit in a mutilated form, and has set a new context for modes of human behaviour. That context increasingly demands an extraordinary level of sexual performance by women in the name of liberation. A popular confessional mode of sexually explicit writing by women circulates a profoundly consistent image of post-liberation for the single woman; her 'liberation' hanging by a thread on the performance of her 'right' to 'sleep around'. Waterstones now keeps a stand for 'Erotic Literature', which is almost exclusively filled with titles by female writers such as 'Over the Knee', 'Exploring the Self', 'All For Lust'. These works have taken on the role of modern romance, substituting *bodily* over *spiritual* states of ecstasy.

Catherine Millett's rather self-conscious *The Sexual Life of Catherine M* is adamant that its author-heroine's actions result from the victories of 'the valiant warriors of the sexual liberation.'[298] Catherine Townsend's less philosophically minded sexual adventuress drones on about the unfairness of the 'double standard' outlasting 'the sexual revolution':

> We've had the sexual revolution – women should feel free to date and have sex like men. Men have always been permitted to sleep around until they find 'The One' so why do women still have to feel sensitive about 'The List'?[299]

It's a good question, and one that might begin to be answered by the fact that she dedicates her account of sexual encounters to her 'mum'. I can't imagine her dedicating a book like this to her daughter, but that may only be a failure of my imagination. Transgression has a firm grasp of the writing female-embodied subject today. Its deep impression can be traced through these confessional, explicit autobiographies of the post-feminist sexual life of (highly literate) women. These narcissistic narratives chart the personal 'adventures' of female-embodied heroines avoiding all limitations to sexual becoming. This is the dream of sexual liberation through transgression realized before our eyes:

> Mine was not the kind of freedom played out on the whims of circumstances, it was a freedom expressed once and for all, an acceptance to abandon oneself unreservedly to a way of life (like a nun saying her vows!)[300]

Our heroine's attempt to liberate herself through unrestrained sexual activity, however, expresses itself as a denial of eroticism. In place of the experiential erotic we find a quantification; a slide from ecstasy to accounting. These post-feminist displays of sexually-liberated life in the end turn on counting, listing, enumerating, collecting and collating multiple sexual encounters. Millet's first chapter is called 'Numbers':

> In the biggest orgies in which I participated ... there could be up to about 150 people (they did not all fuck, some had come to watch), and I would deal with the sex machines of around a quarter or a fifth of them in all available ways: in my hands, my mouth, my cunt and my arse ... Today, I can account for forty-nine men whose sexual organs have penetrated mine and to whom I can attribute a name or, at least, in a few cases, an identity. But I cannot put a number on those that blur into anonymity.[301]

These self-consciously sexual narratives chart a slide from the singularity of the dream of true love towards the multiplicity of encounters that take its place. They open a serious and as yet unanswered question: if not 'the one' then how many?

> There are those who break taboos as powerful as incest. I settled for not having to choose my partners, however many of them there may have been (given the conditions under which I gave myself, if my father had happened to be one of the 'number', I would not have recognized him.)[302]

Millet discovers a 'ready-made philosophy' in Bataille, and a reflection of herself reading *O*:

> Claude told me to read *Histoire d'O* and there were three ways in which I identified with the heroine: I was always ready; my cunt certainly wasn't barred with a chain, but I was sodomized as often as I was taken from the front; and finally, I would have loved her reclusive life in a house isolated from the rest of the world.[303]

The sexual revolution's 'newly converted' to 'the New World of sex' perhaps inevitably fall into believing that 'fucking – and by that I meant fucking frequently and willingly whoever was (or were) the partner (or partners) – was a way of life'.[304] This is a 'play at transgression'.[305] In the end Catherine M does indeed find her 'one' amidst the multitude, and the freeplay of sexual encounters narrows as a result:

> I was very talkative with Jacques at first but then I had to cope, more or less well and anyway belatedly, with the ban imposed on sexual adventures and accounts of these adventures the moment our relationship was perceived and lived as one of love.[306]

Her 'complete free will' exercised in her 'chosen sexual life' is a negative freedom. She is subject to an inexorable 'determinism': 'the determinism of the chain in which one link – one man – links you to another, which links you to a third and so on.'[307]

Both Millet and Townsend acknowledge the structural parallel between their 'free' sexual activity and prostitution: 'The teasing I have had for offering my body so easily but not knowing how to make money out of it!'[308] Is this Madame Edwarda at work, then; giving 'freely' (or being too dumb to charge for) what has historically been marketed by the pimp? Bataille would answer that 'prostitution is the logical consequence of the feminine attitude.'[309] This fall from the possibility of a qualititative experience of liberation into the hell of quantified sexual 'adventures' is unbearable in the longer term. I would still rather suffer the fate of Elizabeth Bennet than that of Catherine Millet. After all, the intensity Millet seems to experience in her extraordinary life of sexual terrorism is described as 'the same torpor I feel waiting at airports.'[310] Lizzy, on the other hand, enjoys the entirely unexpected happy ending she realized she had desired all along:

> Elizabeth was delighted. She had never seen a place for which nature had done more, or where natural beauty had been so little counteracted by an awkward taste. They were all of them warm in their admiration; and at that moment she felt, that to be mistress of Pemberley might be something![311].

If we resist the invitation to think of transgression as a social and individual inevitability and start instead to recognize in it a historically and culturally specific mode of theory, the anguished expression of an unresolved post-Christianity, we can better grasp what is at stake in this discussion. Wolfgang Iser has recently defined theories of the kind applied in literary work as 'intellectual tools'.[312] He differentiates usefully between 'hard-core' and 'soft-core' theories:

> The former – as practised in physics, for instance – makes predictions, whereas the latter – as practised in the humanities – is an attempt at mapping.

Perhaps the most striking technical aspect of transgression as a theory, then, lies in this shift from a descriptive (mapping) to a predictive purpose; a move which (appropriately) turns transgression into 'hard-core' theory. Transgression tends to the prophetic, because it lives in a state of disavowed apocalyptic terror. Situated as it is in the gap left by the individual and collective spiritual disillusionment that permeates contemporary Western consciousness, transgression risks the possibility of retribution:

> WE ARE FEROCIOUSLY RELIGIOUS and, to the extent that our existence is the condemnation of everything that is recognized today, and our inner exigency demands that we be equally imperious . . . It is time to abandon the world of the civilized and its light. It is too late to be reasonable and educated – which has led to a life without appeal. Secretly or not, it is necessary to become completely different, or cease to be.[313]

However, Iser continues:

> it would be meaningless for theoretical inquiries in the humanities to make predictions. Art and literature can be assessed, but not predicted, and one cannot even anticipate the multiple relationships they contain. Prediction aims at mastering something, whereas mapping strives to discern something.

The 'soft-core' theories of the arts find closure not in establishing a law for making predictions, but in the 'introduction of metaphors':

> Metaphor versus law, as the respective 'keystone idea' of soft and hard-core theory, highlights a vital difference between the sciences and the humanities. A law has to be applied, whereas a metaphor triggers associations. The former establishes realities, and the latter outlines patterns.[314]

Transgression has attempted to 'establish a reality' on the basis of a key metaphor for post-Christian thought. Situated in the conscious absence of a sacred reality, the restraint we suffer through secular conventions is experienced as an oppressive interference, making any attempt at transgression a potentially revolutionary act. Recognition of transgressive impulses and of the inextricable relationship between transgression and taboo has quietly converted into an injunction to transgress, reproducing itself through the now rather mainstreamed authority of 'liberational' academic thought. Transgression offers itself as the royal road to liberation and threatens to foreclose this serious and still valuable dream.

There is an important, if subtle, difference between the idea of transgression as 'a dynamic element of society that served to prevent stagnation whilst at the same time maintaining stability' and the assertion that 'transgression of the foundations of Western social life has become a necessity . . .'[315] Michael Richardson notes this shift from apprehending limited, localized and formal transgressions toward the totalizing effect of the concept released from its productive locality, in which 'Bataille's very concrete notion of transgression is completely undermined'.[316]

Transgression, in retrospect, can seem petulant, proceeding from that moment of shocked recognition of the uselessless of a human life, and of the human project in general, to justify living for the intensity of experience alone. Lawrence Schehr argues that: 'To conceive of transgression, crossing the line (or even crossing out the line) is to effectuate a translation, a substitution, a semiotization of the intensity of sexuality.'[317] Transgression and nihilism are the twin poles of post-Christian sensibility.

Transgression is redolent of the adolescence of human conscious-ness, then, if we are willing to accept that ontogeny recapitulates phylogeny. Colette Peignot had already apprehended this petulance as the mark of Bataille's failure to carry his revolutionary project through without compromise. She articulated a brief but powerful analysis of his dependence on prostitutes as a mythification of his self-focused desire:

> The man enters through a small low door, takes several steps and finds himself in a room. He is free of all hindrances
>   then he emerges his face smooth as though purged, he leaves by another door, another street, he goes to the Communist meeting – he will be speaking
>   he who has just bought women, taken part in the monstrous and vile comedy just like that, quite bluntly with perfect contempt. Did he come to these ideas through love or hate? How can these people who respect human rights, respect proletarians, see a prostitute as an instrument of their pleasure? They do not see the woman, the human being, who

comes from who knows where? Oppressed by what or by whom to have come to this point? . . .
 Eroticism as the depths of despair but absolutely incompatible with active, strong life. Playing the worst game of man's disintegration.[318]

A theory that does not 'see the woman' in such a scene is 'incompatible with active, strong life'. Such a theory can only reiterate the core qualities of repressive, autoaffective, post-Enlightenment desire in its shrill claims to a debased freedom. Transgression is the ego's last ditch attempt at the self-defeating prophecy of sovereignty. Kathy Acker is also concerned that liberational theories do not 'see' the woman:

I knew this as a child, before I ever read Plato, Irigaray, Butler. That, as a girl, I was outside the world. I wasn't. I had no name. For me, language was being. There was no entry for me into language. As a receptacle, as a womb, as Butler argues, I could be entered, but I could not enter, and so I could neither have nor make meaning in the world.
 I was unspeakable so I ran into the language of others.[319]

This is the alternative dream of Kathy Acker, of 'the body, my body, which exists outside of patriarchal definitions . . . that is not possible':

But who is any longer interested in the possible? Like Alice, I suspect that the body, as Butler argues, might not be co-equivalent with materiality, that my body might be deeply connected to, if not be, language.
 But what is this language? This language which is not constructed on hierarchical subject-object relations?
 When I dream, my body is the site, not only of the dream, but also of the dreaming and of the dreamer. In other words, in this case or in this language, I cannot separate subject from object, much less from the acts of perception.[320]

Thinking against transgression as a mother has reversed its claims for me. As a conscious maternal subject I am not (only) an object of transgressive desire. I live within and outside that scheme, both subjected to and objectified within it. This is a point on which I concur with Catherine Millet:

You are like a rubber band that has been stretched and then released, and comes back to smack the hand holding it; you are alternately the subject which seizes its environment (even if only by looking at it) and the object which is seized.

I learnt this through pregnancy and writing; she learnt it 'quite unexpectedly, in a sex shop'.[321]

I can acknowledge and comment on my place in the scheme of transgression, but have no way to experience the *desire for* transgression now without forgetting most of myself. The unavoidable object of trangressive desire is a dead mother's body:

> For Bataille as for Sade, the mother is nature's privileged victim ... For Bataille, the mother's sex is the cause of his anguish. The narrative of *Ma Mere* is an account of this dread which culminates in the unveiling of her sexual fantasies. Bataille's fascination for the maternal corpse, his revolting arousal, completes the total degradation of her body. Desire can be fully assumed in Bataille's work on the condition that the mother has become literally matter (*la matiere*).[322] [Lukacher]

Transgression may be so deeply entangled in the formative relationship between the emergent consciousness and the mother's body from which it struggles to individuate that I can access the thought of transgression only by forgetting that I *am* that mother (in the most general sense, the level at which theory operates). Remembering troubles the transgressive imperative.

Transgressive feminism is not really sustainable under conditions of maternity anyway. Sleep becomes more liberating than transgression and random sexual activity has never offered sustainable liberatory possibilities. Liberation has to be fully collective (which would include protecting the children from the voracious desires of miserable adults) or it is nothing. Where should we place the 'limit' to sexual liberation? Incest is only another limit after all.

Bataille explored his own desires through the obscene desires of the mother in *My Mother* (written in 1962, the year of his own death). Lukacher identifies what is at work here with impressive understatement: 'Bataille seems unable to assume the separation from the mother'.[323]

> I found myself lying down in the apartment of my dead mother: her corpse rested in the next room. I was sleeping poorly and remembered that two years before I participated in an orgy in my mother's absence, exactly in her room and in her bed which now was not supporting her corpse. This orgy in the maternal bed took place by chance during my birthday night: my ecstatic motions among my accomplices were interposed between the birth which gave me life and the dead woman for whom I felt then a desperate love. I expressed it several times in terrible, childish sobbings. The extreme voluptuousness of my memories prompted me to go to this orgiastic bedroom to masturbate while looking at the corpse. [Bataille][324]

I can't avoid the fact that I would really rather he had repressed those desires and their expression. Not in the sense that I would censor his speech, deny the truth, and pretend that such desires do not found some fundamental aspect of human consciousness. It's just that there might still be something to be said for a reasonable level of repression, in writing as well as in life. Transgression reaches its climax when it has a dead female body to jerk around with. Acknowledging this desire is one thing; extending it is quite another.

The Sadean-Nietszchean stream of transgressive thought in the wake of the death of God provoked Bataille to explore his own superlative capacity for sustaining transgression in writing. I have brought Lewis's counter-transgressive example to the foreground here to show how the extrapolation of Bataille's thought can 'only exist as a part' of post-war European criticism: 'The proposition that truth is the whole turns out to be identical with its contrary, namely, that in each case it exists only as a part.' [Adorno][325]

> The belief that the truth of a theory is the same as its productiveness is clearly unfounded. There are some, however, who appear to maintain the opposite: that theory has so little need of application in thinking that it should dispense with it entirely. They falsely interpret every utterance as an ultimate avowal, command, or taboo. They would bow down to the idea as to a god, or attack it as if it were an idol. Where ideas are concerned they are completely lacking in freedom. But it is an essential aspect of truth that one should play a part in it as an active subject.

This is a very small and objectively limited example: comparing the thoughts of two white male European intellectuals as if these were the *only* possibles of critical thought was never my intention, and I can identify with neither of them in the end (although I had a lot of fun with Bataille on the way). I only wanted to say that we may have mistaken the sheer intensity of Bataille's life, and the peculiar quality of thought that a life like that can produce when intellectualized, for the truest – because most *anguished* – example of what it might mean to be human. Colette Peignot, who wrote with at least as much beauty and truth, died young. The peasants whose lives she had coveted died most silently of all. It is after all just possible, but I wouldn't want to press the point, that Bataille's model of transgression is itself only the symptom of a syphilitic masculinity: not to be passed on then. If I were his homeopath I would want to prescribe *Mederinum*.

Following the thought of transgression has made me wonder whether much of what we now call 'Theory' is critical surfing in the fascinating wake of Bataille. I had thought I could expose his false premise: his unresolved dependence on female embodiment as the scaffold for his intellectual mirror-gazing. I wanted to show off the parallel concerns and correlations between Lewis's transgressive conservatism and Bataille's conservative transgression. This has left me with a critical hangover which may take some time to pass. I will briefly outline the shape of that hangover here, and then leave you in peace and suffer it in silence.

That hangover is best expressed as an unanswered question: what is it that privileges Bataille's response when compared to the parallel case of Lewis's seduction by a living God, and the moral consciousness this restores to the place of transgression?

> The earliest converts were converted by a single historical fact (the Resurrection) and a single theological doctrine (the Redemption) operating on a sense of sin which they already had – and sin, not against some new fancy-dress law produced as a novelty by a 'great man', but against the old, platitudinous, universal moral law which they had been taught by their nurses and mothers.[326]

'The old, platitudinous, universal moral law . . . taught by their nurses and mothers.' That 'knowledge' associated with 'nurses' and 'mothers' (the implied difference is interesting) so long diminished to fairy tale and romance, encodes something essential to human life and consciousness. What difference does it make that the highly feminized time and space in which this knowledge is imbibed has been diminished in the name of equality? But everything I try to say now sounds like a regression, which was always the danger with this project. How to turn against the tide of transgression without falling back into regression?

Herbert Marcuse produced a compelling summary of the relationship between sexual and general liberation:

> The processes that create the ego and the superego also shape and perpetuate specific societal institutions and relations. Such psychoanalytic concepts as sublimation, identification, and introjection have not only a psychical but also a social content: they terminate in a system of institutions, laws, agencies, things, and customs that confront the individual as objective entities. Within this antagonistic system, the mental conflict between ego and superego, between ego and id, is at one and the same time a conflict between the individual and his society.[327]

He outlined the possibility for a 'non-repressive instinctual order' arising out of 'liberation' achievable through reactivating 'early stages of the libido which were surpassed in the development of the reality ego' dissolving 'the institutions of society in which the reality ego exists':

> It would still be a reversal of the process of civilization, as a consequence not of defeat but of victory in the struggle for existence, and supported by a free society, such liberation might have very different results ... a 'regression' – but in the light of mature consciousness and guided by a new rationality.

The test of his model for imagining 'the possibility of a non-repressive civilization' is, of course, sexuality:

> Non-repressive order is possible only if the sex instincts can, by virtue of their own dynamic and under changed existential and societal conditions, generate lasting erotic relations among mature individuals. We have to ask whether the sex instincts, after the elimination of all surplus-repression, can develop a 'libidinal rationality' which is not only compatible with but even promotes progress toward higher forms of civilized freedom.

His concept of 'non-repressive civilization' is a seductive paradox. It reaches for Christian imagery to capture the point:

> Man would order his life in accordance with his fully developed knowledge, so that he would ask again what is good and what is evil. If the guilt accumulated in the civilized domination of man by man can ever be redeemed by freedom, then the 'original sin' must be committed again: 'We must again eat from the tree of knowledge in order to fall back into the state of innocence'.[328]

Marcuse noted with chilling calm that 'the emergence of a non-repressive reality principle involving instinctual liberation would *regress* behind the attained level of civilized rationality ... instinctual liberation is a relapse into barbarism.'[329] He also imagined, however, that '[o]ccurring at the height of civilization, as a consequence not of defeat but of victory in the struggle for existence, and supported by a free society, such liberation might have very different results':

> It would still be a reversal of this process of civilization, a subversion of culture – but *after* culture had done its work and created the mankind and the world that could be free.

It's a lovely thought, but leaves me with the sharp conviction that we have not quite managed to build 'the world that could be free'. It might be respectful to show a little more restraint in our critical ambitions. A return to the possibility of a 'platitudinous universal moral law' is another way of thinking about the freedom of restraint. The closest we might come to it now is the freefall of the early stages of love (or a state of Grace), where the world seems appeased for a while and shows no resistance to the interpenetrating and mutually enabling desires of the subjects of love.

The Sadean-Nietszchean stream of critical thought, and the fetishizing of dominance this engenders, was answered differently by Adorno and Horkheimer's *Dialectic of Enlightenment*:

> The formalization of reason is only the intellectual expression of mechanized production. The means is fetishized, and absorbs pleasure ... Domination survives as an end in itself, in the form of economic power.[330]

Transgression has revealed itself to be an almost exclusively masculine critical preoccupation. Transgression as a respected *intellectual* tradition is the domain of male white Europeans. De Sade – Nietszche – Bataille – Foucault; an auto-affective genealogy that has incorporated otherness in the form of female bodies and female-embodied thought as the material resistance against which it forces its intellectual climax in a repetitive gesture that returns to the point of departure without the possibility of what Luce Irigaray – for whom 'woman represents the emergence of the other with respect to Western tradition' – would call 'horizontal transcendence'.[331] If 'Transgression' cannot be thought *by* the other, but only thinks of itself in violent domination or incorporation of otherness, through which it reaches its climax of auto-affective intensity, it can only really represent the logic of the same masquerading as a radical break with tradition.

To make overt the core metaphor on which the theory of transgression attempts to close itself as a system is quite possible. Schehr explains that Lyotard, in his writing encounter with Bataille, had 'a raging hard-on'; his 'intensities gone wild':

> There is a homoerotic subtext of anal penetration ... [c]ircles of men then ... [i]ntensities of prostitution, homosexuality, ultimately equivalent ... an orgy of exchange ... homosexual fellation: a cosmic circle jerk.[332]

I wonder if the 'intensities' of prostitution really are equivalent to homosexuality? It seems very unlikely, unless Schehr means the intellectual prostitution of homosexual desires. In any case, this intellectual figure of a 'cosmic circle jerk' by necessity excludes women except as *objects* – rather than reciprocal subjects – of representation or thought. Women would break the circle. Julia Kristeva has already noted that Bataille explores openly the 'subject/object relationship (and not subject/other subject)' that is 'rooted in anal eroticism'.[333] Now, I've nothing against 'anal eroticism' in itself, but wonder whether this is the best – or only – way we might order our critical work. Anal sex, incidentally, features heavily in female-authored transgressive literature, as the sign of a female-embodied experience of bisexuality:

> I can see myself at the foot of a very narrow staircase, in the rue Quincampoix, hesitating before deciding to go up. Claude and I were given the address by chance. We didn't know anyone. The apartment was very dark with a low ceiling. I could hear men nearby putting the word about, whispering: 'She wants it up the arse', or warning someone heading the wrong way: 'No, she only takes it from behind.' That particular time it did at the end hurt. But I also had the personal satisfaction of having had no feelings of restraint.[334]

Kathy Acker knew that for de Sade women can 'transform (...) themselves into men by choosing to engage in sodomy': 'In sodomy, the most delicious position is the passive one. In other words, a woman can know freedom by choosing to counterfeit a man who selects the bottom power position.'[335] I'm not convinced by this model of freedom: it seems rather limiting for women to counterfeit the freedom of homosexual men. If criticism is personal to the point of performing unconscious desires, it should also be possible to direct the process in accordance with some form of moral consciousness (restraint) without capitulating to regressive tendencies or reducing desire to instrumentalized productivity. This section takes the form of a 'Preface to Compassion' against 'Transgression' as an experiment in shifting the discussion beyond the transgression/regression impasse. If transgression overcomes the other in its drive to achieve a sovereign state of continuity, intensified by breaches in a fundamental moral ground for human individuation, compassion might just offer an equally bracing model of radical liberation, and one less jarring to maternal subjectivity.

Adorno was clear about one thing. The acknowledged enemy of Sadean-Nietzschean transgression is compassion:

> Whoever surrenders to compassion 'perverts the general law: whence it results that pity, far from being a virtue, becomes a real vice once it leads us to interfere with an inequality prescribed by nature's laws.' Sade and Nietzsche recognized that, after the formalization of reason, pity still remained as, so to speak, the sensual consciousness of the identity of the general and the particlar, as naturalized mediation.

Compassion is labelled 'womanly and childish' by Sade's model heroine of transgression, who

> boasts of her 'stoicism,' the 'serene command over the emotions' which allows her 'to do, and to continue to do, everything without any feeling.'

Compassion is 'a weakness, born of fear and misfortune, a weakness which must above all be overcome when one strives to suppress the excessive sensitivity which is irreconcilable with the maxims of philosophy.' And, as if it needed further emphasis: 'Woman is the source of "outbreaks of unrestrained compassion." '[336]

Compassion is the 'enemy' of transgression in the simple sense that compassion recognizes the irreducible truth of the other in any encounter, critical or otherwise, while transgression centres on the inner experience of a sovereign will-to-power; masterhood. Angela Carter's searing analysis of de Sade exposes the particular condition of Sadean transgression as the denial of the possibility of love: 'The libertine's perversions are the actings-out of his denial of love'.[337] The maternal body is the primary object of transgression because transgression is always regressive in its tendencies, pushing back the ordering injunctions of the fundamental, maternal 'architecture' that structures the subject's individuation.

> The excremental enthusiasm of the libertines transforms the ordure in which they roll to a bed of roses. The pleasure of the libertine philosophers derives in a great part from the knowledge they have overcome their initial disgust. By the exercise of the will, they have overcome repugnance and so, in one sense, are liberated from the intransigence of reality. This liberation from reality is their notion of freedom.[338] [Carter]

Transgression situates itself squarely in the abject, converting feelings of horror and disgust into 'libidinal intensities':

> [Bataille] chose immanence over transcendence, evil over good, the useless over the useful, disorder over order, contagion over immunisation, expenditure over capitalisation, the immediate over ends, the present over the future (and the instant over time), glory over power, impulse over calculation, madness over reason, limitless prodigality over subjection to parsimony, the subject over the object, being over salvation, communication over separation.[339]

Transgression has revealed an abiding longing for 'continuity' glimpsed in 'limit conditions' outside of the range of reason. This is an enduring and valuable insight, which has emerged from a profound intellectual reflection on the mind-body continuum, demonstrating how 'limit' experiences of the body can produce exciting new states of mind. It is conceivable, however, that the 'limit' states preoccupying critical transgression to date demonstrate only a very small part of the story that might be told concerning the mind-body continuum:

> The main thrust of Western intellectual history has avoided the discussion of the perfected human being. The focus has rather been on the universal, not the exceptional ... today's Western thinkers [are] more open to discussing the exceptional than were their predecessors, but, oddly, they examine mainly the negative side, that of the abnormal or diseased. Modern Western neurophysiology and psychoanalysis have opened the door to the extraordinary in human life, but only, as it were, the back door of the subnormal instead of the front door of the supernormal.[340]

Transgression is fixated on the publicly abjected extremities of human potential: madness, orgies, murder, rape, incest, ecstacy, s-m, death. Michel Foucault, according to James Miller, generated his most interesting ideas through experimenting with 'unusual bodily sensations and altered states of consciousness'.[341] Miller identifies the inspiration for Foucault's mature intellectual work as an LSD trip in California. His companion on the trip recalls that at its height, with tears 'streaming down his cheeks', Foucault suddenly exclaimed: 'I now understand my sexuality'.[342] His sexuality was certainly very interesting, as was indeed Bataille's. But there is no reason for those very particular (and in the most practical sense 'limited') 'limit' experiences to become definitive of the range and direction of critical thought to follow.

The model of sovereign liberation forcing its way through transgression may turn out in the long run to have been a retrograde step:

> the conquest of morality and aesthetics, of shame, disgust and fear, the pursuit of greater and greater sexual sophistication in terms of private sensation lead them directly to the satisfactions of the child; transgression becomes regression and, like a baby, they play with their own excrement. [Carter][343]

Nick Hocking was the first to suggest to me that there are 'many parallels between [Bataille and Tibetan Tantric Sadhana] in such areas as the emptiness of the individual subject, the limits of language and the limits of consciousness, and the death of God'.[344] This affinity offers a possibility that our critical inheritance of Bataillean transgression has simply been foreclosed by the failure of critical consciousness to follow through the extraordinarily possible thought of the 'death of God'. Transgression remains trapped in the anguish of the act of mind that knows it has killed this idea.

Transgression in Bataille's mode approaches the experience of 'emptiness' by its emphasis on the non-substantial, inner experience, 'fusion' and non-action:

> If one wants to represent, with an initial clarity, the 'grail' obstinately pursued through successive, deceptive, and cloudy depths, it is necessary to insist upon the fact that it could never have been a *substantial* reality; on the contrary, it was an element characterized by the impossibility of its enduring. The term *privileged instant* is the only one that, with a certain amount of accuracy, accounts for what can be encountered *at random* in the search; the opposite of a *substance* that withstands the test of time, it is something that flees as soon as it is seen and cannot be grasped.[345]

'Emptiness', however, once experienced, is for the practitioner of 'ultimate liberation', not an end in itself:

> The insight into emptiness, facilitated by awareness, leads to an empowered compassion. The relationship between such insight and concern for others is an important principle in Mahayana Buddhism. Insight, and its affective counterpart, compassion, are crucial for the Buddhist enterprise of ultimate liberation. [Klein][346]

The mode of liberation promised by transgression is *always* limited, momentary, fleeting, unsatisfactory:

> Orgasm has possessed the libertine; during the irreducible timelessness of the moment of orgasm, the hole in the world through which we fall, he has been as a god, but this state is as fearful as it is pleasurable and, besides, is lost as soon as it is attained. He has burst into the Utopia of desire, in which only the self exists; he has not negotiated the terms of his arrival there, as gentle lovers do, but taken Utopia by force. See, the conquering hero comes. And, just as immediately, he has been expelled from it, a fall like Lucifer's, from heaven to hell. [Carter][347]

By contrast, the 'ultimate liberation' offered through experience of 'emptiness', and the capacity for radical compassion it engenders, is unlimited by external conditions. It cannot be thwarted by the counter-desire of the other or the resistance of the object; it does not struggle to define itself against the constraints of necessity ('reality'); and it is not, according to Bataille, limited by 'the idea of a personal God.'[348] Perhaps most importantly for this discussion, emptiness-compassion does not remain bound to an ambivalent desire for the (dead) maternal body as the ground of its becoming. Compassion is instead *actively* generated by the practice of imagining the other *as* the subject's living mother:

> Imagine your mother clearly in front of you ... As your mother, she protected you from all harm and provided you all benefit and happiness. Particularly in this lifetime she carried you for a long time in her womb. Then, when you were a helpless, newborn infant, she held you to the warmth of her flesh and bounced you on the tips of her ten fingers. She suckled you at her breast ... and used her hand to wipe your excrement. So in various ways she nurtured you tirelessly ... Even more, what she gave to you were not things that she had obtained easily but that she had received through great hardship ... In short, contemplate one-pointedly how your mother provided help and happiness and cleared away harm and suffering to the best of her knowledge and ability.[349]

It's not supposed to be an easy exercise. Just the first step of imagining your personal mother's particular sacrifices to generate, sustain and nurture the life of the subject you became is more difficult than it sounds on first reading. Close your eyes and try it for a moment. It will take a few goes to settle into the practice, and the results can be nauseating at first. Extending the feelings of compassion that result to the people closest to you is just about possible. Taking this further to apply those feelings to those you dislike or 'hate' and to the millions to whom you feel nothing much at all takes serious and sustained practice. The effects on the practising subject can be very interesting, but vary from person to person, so it is best to experiment rather than be told what to feel.

The mode of emptiness-compassion I want to offer up against transgression is not a sentimental, sickly emphasis on suffering. It is the spontaneous selflessness that flows from an acknowledgement of the 'emptiness' of the 'self': and in this sense extends the thought of 'continuity' without linking it to its transgressive concomitants, 'sacrifice' and 'anguish'. This idea might accept and complete the transgression of thought that Bataille attempted to put into motion through his work; acknowledging 'the absence of reified selfhood' without falling from there into the lazy nihilism of much critical transgression.[350]

Emptiness-compassion begins from the moment of realization that the self is not reifiable and does not exist 'inherently':

The conclusion that the self does not exist at all is not drawn, but rather that the self is utterly unreifiable, non-inherently existent. Understanding this emphasizes the contingent, dependent, interconnected, and non-autonomous nature of the self's existence.

The self apprehended in emptiness-compassion theory is 'associated with the development of a compassionate sense of relatedness in which self and other are seen not as oppositional but as relative designations, like the far and near banks of a river' [Klein][351]:

> By becoming accustomed to the equality of self and other,
> The spirit of enlightenment becomes firm.
> Self and other are interdependent.
> Like this side and the other side of a river, they are false.
>
> The other bank is not in itself 'other';
> In relation to someone else it is 'this bank.'
> Similarly, 'self' does not exist in its own right;
> In relation to someone else it is 'other'.[352]

Emptiness theory refers to the initial awareness that 'self and other are merely posited in relation to a particular reference point and do not essentially exist'.[353] This much is already familiar from several strands of Western thought, including critical transgression.

A strong concept of emptiness has manifested in the recent, controversial, 'spiritual turn' of Critical Realism:

> When someone is trained or intuitively develops the capacity to experience non-dual states they are accessing one's 'ground-state' (one's essential or transcendentally real self). Being in one's ground-state is to become maximally aware of the here, the now, of one's responsibility for oneself and society and of co-presence in a way that fosters an effective individual within the collective. Experiencing co-presence within one's ground-state creates an affinity or care entailing a reciprocality that orients 'right-action'. According to Bhaskar this is because a basic characteristic of fine structure is the good of being (generically referred to as love). Thus to be in one's ground-state and to engage in right-action is to act in terms of an implicit non-calculative and nurturing valuation of being ... ground-states by definition are incompatible with commodified, fetishistic and instrumental relations with others and also with transference behaviours like consumerism.[354]

For late CR, focusing on and practising the experience of 'non-dual' states accesses the emptiness of inherent existence, and leads *inevitably* to a 'reciprocality' that forms the basis of 'right-action'. As a result, 'the issue is not to engage in a study of society' but to develop an awareness that the alienated world in fact depends upon free, loving, creative, intelligent energy and that in becoming aware of this we begin the process of transforming the oppressive structures we have produced.[355]

In another register, Luce Irigaray has recently written openly of her God as 'the transfer of the other into the beyond':

> As invisible, he acts as guarantor of alterity as such . . . a God who keeps his freedom in spite of our call, except sometimes because of compassion, a God who escapes our gaze and our hold, truly seems to be the guarantor of the memory that the other exists. God is waiting for our encountering and entering into relation with him, or her.[356]

Perhaps most influential to date, Slavoj Žižek has drawn heavily on emptiness theory in the concluding pages of his recent book, *The Parallax View*, to argue that the 'dynamic of "virtual capitalism", rather than oppressing us, confronts us with' the 'nonsubstantial character of reality'.[357] He comments here that:

> the only 'critical' lesson to be drawn from the Buddhist perspective about today's virtual capitalism is that we should be aware that we are dealing with a mere theatre of shadows, with insubstantial virtual entities, and, as a result, that we should not fully engage ourselves in the capitalist game, that we should play the game with an inner distance. Virtual capitalism could thus act as a first step toward liberation.

For Slavoj Žižek, 'liberation' results from the realization that 'the cause of our suffering and enslavement is not objective reality itself (there is no such thing) but our Desire, our craving for material things, our excessive attachment to them.' His response to this realization is too glib to get us very far:

> All we have to do, after we rid ourselves of the false notion of substantialist reality, is thus to renounce our desire itself, to adopt an attitude of inner peace and distance.

Renunciation of desire is no simple thing in practice, however, and arguably more suited to the life of a well-paid, highly reflective philosopher than of most subjects suffering the disorientating effects of virtual capitalism in their daily lives. But we do have to start somewhere, and where we are is always the best place.

It is quite possible to accept insight into the longing expressed through transgression without making such a song-and-dance about its more mutilated, anguished expressions. It is also possible (if not ultimately inevitable) to experience this longed-for continuity without creating conditions of anguish and without entering the states of moral transgression which are favoured by the Bataillean school. This is what Kathy Acker realized in facing her own death consciously:

> I have become interested in languages which I cannot *make up*, which I cannot *create* or even *create in*: I have become interested in languages which I can only come upon (as I disappear), a pirate upon buried treasure. The dreamer, the dreaming, the dream.[358]

I think that Joy Davidman expresses the thought I am chasing here rather beautifully. She probably deserves, and would not expect to have, the last word:

> O agony, burn at my heart;
> Burn at my heart and keep me warm.
> Deliver me from the harsh iron of winter,
> Unclothe me of the silver fur of frost,
> Pare away the ice from the ends of my fingers.
> Set me free of cold idleness
> And deliver me from the barrier across my tongue
> For I will say my word.
> This is winter and I am imprisoned in it
> With the tips of my fingers slowly turning to ice
> But I shall not forget words
> And the beautiful ringing of words linked together,
> And I shall remember compassion
> And keep the heart lit with a fire of pain
> And let the sound of suffering made music
> Whistle and sing in my throat until I die.[359]

Appendix:
Timeline of Transgression

C16th

Drouin, Daniel. (1595) Sieur de Bel Endroit. *Les Vengeances divines de la transgression des sainctes ordonnances de Dieu, selon l'ordre des dix commandemens.* Paris.

C17th

Murton, John. (1620) *A Description of what God hath predestined concerning Man, in his creation, transgression, & regeneration. As also an answere to John Robinson touching baptism.* London.

Coppe, Abiezer. (1651) *A Remonstrance of the sincere and zealous Protestation of Abiezer Coppe, against the blasphemous and execrable opinions recited in the Act of Aug. 10. 1650. The breach whereof, the author hath – through mistake – been missuspected of . . . Or, Innocence – clouded with the name of transgression – wrapt up in silence, etc.* London: James Cottrel.

Burrough, Edward, of the Society of Friends. (1657) *A Description of the State and Condition of all Mankinde upon the face of the whole Earth. And a discovery unto all; shewing what man was in his creation before transgression, and what he is in transgression... Also, the way of restoration ... is here declared unto all the sons and daughters of Adam, etc.* London: Giles Calvert.

Woodrow, Thomas. (1659). *A Brief Relation of the State of Man Before Transgression... With a word to the gathered people in Melcombe, etc.* London: Thomas Simmons.

Shewen, William. (1675). *A Few Words concerning Conscience, what it is, and what estate it was in before transgression. And how it became darkened...and corrupted. And how again it may be enlightened...and set at liberty, etc.* London.

C18th

Remarks upon Mr. Hodges's pamphlet entitul'd Corah's transgression in murmuring against Aaron ... By a lay-man of the Presbyterian persuasion. Belfast. 1711.

Whitney, Peter, the elder. (1774) *The transgression of a land punished by a multitude of rulers, considered in two discourses, etc.* Boston, Mass.

C19th

Winks, Joseph Foulkes. (1829)[Choice pieces, etc.] *The Bull Running at Stamford, a transgression of the Divine Laws ... Being the substance of a sermon ... With an appendix containing accounts of the origin of this custom, etc.* London: G. Wightman.

Townsend, George, Canon of Durham. (1845). *The Transgression and Punishment of Uzziah.* A sermon. In Watson, A. Practical Sermons, Vol. 1.8°.

Blessed is he whose Transgression is forgiven. London, 1854.

Zola, Émile (1886). *Abbe Mouret's Transgression. A realistic novel.* London: Vizetelly & Co.

Lanza, Clara Hammond. (n.d.) *Basil Morton's transgression: A novel* by Marquise Clara Lanza. Research Publications. Originally published 1889, New York: Minerva Publishing Co.

Vallings, Harold. (1893) *The Transgression of Terence Clancy.* 3 vol. London: R. Bentley & Son.

Oppenheim, Paul, of Berlin-Lichterfelde. (1896) *Das Alttertiar der Colli Berici in Venetien, due Stellung der Schichten von Priabona und die oligocane Transgression in alpinen Europa, etc.* With 4 plates.

Thorburn, Septimus Smet. (1899) *Transgression. A novel.* C. A. Pearson: London.

C20th

(1900–1910)

Carryl, Guy Wetmore. (1904) *The Transgression of Andrew Vane. A novel.* New York: H. Holt & Co.

Dale, Darley, pseud. [i.e. Francesca Maria Steele.] (1907) *Naomi's Transgression.* With original illustrations by Harold Piffard. London & New York: Frederick Warne & Co.

Leiviska, Iivari Gabriel. (1909) *Zu den Küstenfragen. I. Über die Entstehung der Haupttypen der finnischen Küsten, die höchste marine Grenze und die Transgression des Ancylussees und des Litorinameeres.* Helsingfors.

(1911–1920)

—

(1921–1930)

Vere, Tyler G. (1922) *Children of Transgression*. London.

(1931–1940)

Macdonnell, Eva M. (1935) *Transgression*. A novel. London: Houghton Publishing Co.

Paul, Henry. (1937) *Die Transgression der Visestufe am Nordrande des Rheinischen Schiefergebirges, etc.* pp. 117. pl. 3. Berlin.

Marlière, René. (1939) *La Transgression albienne et cenomanienne dans le Hainaut. Etudes paleontologiques et stratigraphiques.* Memoires du Musee Royal d'Histoire Naturelle de Belgique. no. 89. pp. 440. pl. VIII. Brussels.

(1941–1950)

—

(1951–1960)

—

(1961–1970)

Craig, Barbara M., ed. (1968) *La creacion, La Transgression and L'expulsion of the Mistere du Viel Testament.* Edited by Barbara M. Craig. Lawrence: University of Kansas.

(1971–1980)

Adler, Alfred and Michel Carty. (1971) *La transgression et sa derision.* In: L'Homme. tom. 11. no. 3. pp. 5–63.

Tanner, Tony. (1979) *Adultery in the novel: contract and transgression.* Baltimore, London: John Hopkins University Press.

Moffat, A. J. (1980) *The Plio-Pleistocene transgression in the northern part of the London Basin: a re-examination.* London: University of London.

(1981–1990)

Filteau, Claude. (1981) *Le statut narrative de la transgression: essais sur Hamilton et Beckford.* Sherbrooke, Quebec: Editions Naaman.

Izard, M. and P. Smith, (eds.) (1982) *Between belief and transgression: structuralist essays in religion, history, and myth.* Translation of: *La fonction symbolique,* translated by John Leavitt; with an introduction by James A. Boon. Chicago; London: University of Chicago Press.

Lemert, Charles C. and Garth Gillan. (1982) *Michel Foucault: social theory and transgression.* New York; Guildford: Columbia University Press.

Morale et Transgression: Congres: Selected papers. [1982]

Vaucher Gravili, Anne de. (1982) *Loi et transgression: les histoires tragiques au XVII siecle.* Lecce: Milella.

Lightfoot, P. (1983) *Transgression of dynamic stability thresholds during a transient in a once-through boiler: Numel code application and experimental validation.* Marchwood: Central Electricity Generating Board Technology Planning and Research Division.

Stallybrass, Peter and Allon White. (1986) *The politics and poetics of transgression.* London: Methuen.

Day, Leroy Thomas. (1988) *Narrative transgression and the foregrounding of language in selected prose works of Poe, Valery, and Hofmannsthal.* New York; London: Garland.

Deviance et transgression dans la litterature et les arts britanniques: colloque (1989) colloque organisé par le Groupe d'études et de recherches britanniques de l'Université de Bordeaux III; sous la direction de Michel Jouve et Marie-Claire Royer. Bordeaux: Maison des sciences de l'homme dAquitaine.

Conference (1989). *Gothic fictions: prohibition/transgression: Seminar: Conference: Papers. Gothic fictions 1985.* Toronto, Canada: AMS Press.

Edwards, Catharine. (1989) *Transgression and control: studies in ancient Roman immorality.* Cambridge: Cambridge University Press.

Toumson, Roger. (1989) *La transgression des couleurs: litterature et langage des Antilles: XVIIIe, XIXe, XXe siecles.* Paris: Editions Caribeennes.

Waever, Ole. (1989) *Tradition and transgression in international relations: a post-Ashleyan position.* Copenhagen: Centre for Peace and Conflict Research.

(1991–2000)

Booker, M. Keith. (1991) *Techniques of subversion in modern literature: transgression, abjection, and the carnivalesque.* Gainesville, FL: University of Florida Press.

Kassem, Rania. (1991) *Transgression and unity: language of Oscar Wilde.* University of Strathclyde.

Kramer, Selma and Salman Akhtar, (eds.) (1991) *The Trauma of transgression: psychotherapy of incest victims: 21st Annual Margaret S Mahler symposium on child development: Papers:. The Trauma of transgression Conference May 1990, Philadelphia PA.* Northvale, N.J: J. Aronson.

Porter, Dennis. (1991) *Haunted journeys: desire and transgression in European travel writing.* Princeton, N.J.; Oxford: Princeton University Press.

Tatlock, Lynne, ed. (1991) *Writing on the line: transgression in early modern German literature = Variationen zur Literatur im Umbruch: Grenzuberschreitungen in der deutschen Literatur der Fruhen Neuzeit.* Rodopi: Amsterdam.

Armitt, Lucie Joy. (1992) *Pushing back the limits: the fantastic as transgression in contemporary women's fiction.* University of Warwick.

Cusset, Monique D. (1992) *Mythe et histoire: le pouvoir & la transgression dans l'oeuvre de Rabelais.* Paris: Guy Tredaniel.

Schmid, Thomas H. (1992) *Humor and transgression in Peacock, Shelly, and Byron: a cold carnival.* Lampeter: Lewiston, N.Y: Edwin Mellen.

Serge, Bouez. (1992) *La déesse apaisée: norme et transgression dans l'hindouisme au Bengale.* Paris: Editions de l'Ecole des hautes etudes en sciences sociales.

Cain, Maureen and Christine B. Harrington, (eds.) (1993) *Lawyers in a postmodern world: translation and transgression.* Open University Press.

Chessid, Ilona. (1993) *Thresholds of desire: authority and transgression in the Rougon-Macquart.* New York: Peter Lang.

Classen, Albrecht, (ed.) (1993) *Canon and canon transgression in mediaeval German literature.* Goppingen: Kummerle.

Jasper, David, (ed.) (1993) *Translating Religious Texts: Translation, Transgression and Interpretation.* London: Macmillan.

Martens, Didier. (1993) Une esthetique de la *Transgression*: le vase grec de la fin de l'epoque geometrique au debut de l'epoque classique. Brussels: Academie royale de Belgique.

Scott, Bradfield. (1993) *Dreaming revolution: transgression in the development of American romance.* Iowa City: University of Iowa Press.

Wesley, Marilyn C. (1993) *Refusal and transgression in Joyce Carol Oates' fiction.* Contributions in women studies; no 135. Greenwood Press.

Gilbert, Pamela K. (1994) *Circulation and contagion: transgression and popular novels by Victorian women.* Los Angeles: Faculty of the Graduate School, University of Southern California.

Gregg, John. (1994) *Maurice Blanchot and the literature of transgression.* Princeton, N.J.; Chichester: Princeton University Press.

Hawke, Simon. (1994) *The patrian transgression.* New York; London: Pocket.

Kucich, John. (1994) *The power of lies: transgression in Victorian fiction.* Ithaca, London: Cornell University Press.

Nesteruk, Peter. (1994) *Referentiality and transgression: representations of incest and child sexual abuse in American literature of the twentieth century.* University of Nottingham.

Allison, David B., Mark S. Roberts and Allen S. Weiss, (eds.) (1995) *Sade and the narrative of transgression.* Cambridge: Cambridge University Press.

Gibbons, Frances Vargas. (1995) *Transgression and self-punishment in Isaac Bashevis Singer's searches.* Twentieth century American Jewish writers; vol. 6 New York: Lang.

Lashgari, Deirdre, (ed.) (1995) *Violence, silence, and anger: women's writing as transgression.* Charlottesville; London: University Press of Virginia.

Levesque, Andree. (1995) *Resistance et transgression: etudes en histoire des femmes au Quebec.* Montreal: Editions du Remue-Menage.

San Juan, Epifanio. (1985) *Hegemony and strategies of transgression: essays in cultural studies and comparative literature.* Albany: State University of New York Press.

Spence, Jo. (1995) *Cultural sniping: the art of transgression.* London: Routledge.

Weaver, John C. (1995) *Crimes, constables, and courts: order and transgression in a Canadian city, 1816–1970.* Montreal; London: McGill-Queen's University Press.

Bayles, Martha. (1996) *Ain't that a shame? censorship and the culture of transgression.* London: University of London, Institute of United States Studies.

Cresswell, Tim. (1996) *In place/out of place: geography, ideology, and transgression.* Minneapolis; London: University of Minnesota Press.

Ferla, Kleopatra. (1996) *Von Homers Achill zur Hekabe des Euripides: das Phänomen der Transgression in der griechischen Kultur.* Munchen: Tuduv.

Lee, Hsiao-Hung. (1996) *"Possibilities of hidden things": narrative transgression in Victorian fictional autobiographies.* New York: Peter Lang.

Tierney-Tello, Mary Beth. (1996) *Allegories of transgression and transformation: experimental fiction by women writing under dictatorship.* Albany: State University of New York Press.

Braendlin E.B. and Braendlin Hans P. (eds) (1996) *Authority and transgression in literature and film. 18th Literature and film Conference 1993: (Tallahassee, Fl).* Gainesville: University Press of Florida.

Victor Millet. (ed.) (1996) *Norm und Transgression in deutscher Sprache und Literatur: Kolloquium in Santiago de Compostela, 4–7, Oktober 1995.* Munchen: Iudicium.

Bixler, Jacqueline Eyring. (1997) *Convention and transgression: the theatre of Emilio Carballido.* Lewisburg, PA: Bucknell University Press; London: Associated University Presses.

Highwater, Jamake. (1997) *The mythology of transgression: homosexuality as metaphor.* New York; Oxford: Oxford University Press.

Bradshaw, Penelope Joyce Elizabeth. (1998) *Unsex'd women: the politics of transgression in the poetry of Anna Laetitia Barbauld and Charlotte Smith.* University of Lancaster.

Duffy, Larry and Adrian Tudor, (eds.) (1998) *Les lieux interdits: transgression and French literature.* Hull: University of Hull Press.

McCracken, Peggy. (1998) *The romance of adultery: queenship and sexual transgression in Old French literature.* Philadelphia: University of Pennsylvania Press.

Noakes, Richard John. (1998) *'Cranks and visionaries': science, spiritualism and transgression in Victorian Britain.* University of Cambridge.

Powell, Carolyn Anna. (1998) *The secular sacred: sex, transgression and the numinous in popular vampire fiction.* University of Southampton.

Pun, Ngai. (1998) *Becoming Dagongmei: body, identity and transgression in reform China.* University of London.

Weiner, Andrew D. and Leonard V. Kaplan, (eds.) Weiner, Sonja H. (assoc. ed.) (1998) *Transgression, punishment, responsibility, forgiveness: studies in culture, law and the sacred.* Madison: University of Wisconsin Law School.

Arthurs, Jane and Jean Grimshaw, (eds.) (1999) *Women's bodies: discipline and transgression.* London: Cassell.

Loretelli, Rosamaria and Roberto De Romanis, (eds.) (1999) *Narrating transgression: representations of the criminal in early modern England.* Frankfurt am Main: Peter Lang.

Neuenhaus-Luciano, Petra. (1999) *Individualisierung und Transgression: die Spur Batailles im Werk Foucaults.* Pfaffenweiler: Centaurus.

Benthien C. & I.M. Kruger-Furhoff (hrsg) (1999) *Uber Grenzen: Limitation und Transgression in Literatur und Ästhetik.* Stuttgart: Metzler.

C21st

Hahn, Thomas, (ed.) (2000) *Robin Hood in popular culture: violence, transgression, and justice. From conference: Playing with transgression:*

cultural transformations of Robin Hood (1997 Oct: Rochester, NY). Woodbridge, Suffolk: D.S. Brewer.

Palmer, Bryan D. (2000) *Cultures of darkness: night travels in the histories of transgression.* New York: Monthly Review Press.

Hajduk, Stefan. (2000) *Die Figur des Erhabenen: Robert Musils asthetische Transgression der Moderne.* Wurzburg: Konigshausen & Neumann.

Oates, Leah. (2000) *Transgression.* Chicago: Rhino Press.

Sargisson, Lucy. (2000) *Utopian bodies and the politics of transgression.* London: Routledge.

Souffrant, Eddy M. (2000) *Formal transgression: John Stuart Mill's Philosophy of International Affairs.* Lanham; Oxford: Rowman & Littlefield Publishers.

Abassi, Ali. (2001) *Stendhal hybride: poetique du desordre et de la transgression dans Le rouge et le noir et La chartreuse de Parme.* Paris: Harmattan.

Braziel, Jana Evans and Kathleen LeBesco, (eds.) (2001) *Bodies out of bounds: fatness and transgression.* Berkeley: University of California Press.

Oates, Joyce Carol. (2003) *Faithless: tales of transgression.* London: Fourth Estate.

Eberle, Roxanne. (2001) *Chastity and transgression in women's writing, 1792–1897: interrupting the Harlot's Progress.* Basingstoke: Palgrave.

Harris, Keith Daniel. (2001) *Transgression and mundanity: the global extreme metal music scene.* London: University of London PhD thesis.

Maddern, Carole Anne. (2001) *Female mobility in medieval English romance: a study of travel and transgression.* London, University of London PhD thesis.

Chihaia, Matei. (2002) *Institution und Transgression: inszenierte Opfer in Tragödien Racines und Corneilles.* Tubingen: Narr, 2002. (Originally presented as the author's thesis, Ludwig-Maximilians-Universitat, Munchen, 2000).

Chessex, Jacques. (2002) *Jacques Chessex: transcendance et transgression: entretiens avec Genevieve Bridel.* Lausanne: La Bibiotheque des arts.

Garvey, Pauline Anne. (2002) *Decorative Order: normativity and transgression in the Norwegian home.* London: University of London, PhD thesis.

Jackson, Michael. (2002) *The politics of storytelling: violence, transgression, and intersubjectivity.* Copenhagen: Museum Tusculanum Press.

Raghunath, Anita Shanti. (2002) *Discourses of Carnival and Transgression in British and Caribbean Writing.* London: University of London, PhD thesis.

Universite de Clermont-Ferrand II. Groupe interdisciplinaire d'etude du XVIIIe siecle. (2002) *Normes et transgression au XVIIIe siecle*

Textes reunis par Pierre Dubois. Paris: Presses de l'universite de Paris-Sorbonne.

Jenks, Chris. (2003) *Transgression*. London: Routledge.

Serfaty, Anne. (2003) Les *'Vilaines nouveautez' de Pigault-Lebrun (1753–1835): l'ecriture populaire, de la transgression a la reception*. Exeter: University of Exeter, PhD thesis.

Kittredge, Katharine, (ed.) (2003) *Lewd & notorious: female transgression in the eighteenth century*. Ann Arbor, Mich.: University of Michigan Press.

Barron, Lee. (2004) *The figure of the angel as postmodern icon: angels and the transgression of boundaries within contemporary cinema*. Sunderland: University of Sunderland.

Best, Ulrich. (2004) *German-Polish cross-border co-operation and the politics of transgression*. Plymouth: University of Plymouth, PhD thesis.

Classen, Albrecht, (ed.) (2004) *Discourses on love, marriage, and transgression in medieval and early modern literature*. Tempe, Ariz: Arizona Center for Medieval and Renaissance Studies.

Howe, Linda S. (2004) *Transgression and conformity: Cuban writers and artists after the Revolution*. Madison, Wis.; London: University of Wisconsin Press.

Albers, Irene & Helmut Pfeiffer (eds) (2004) *Michel Leiris: Szenen der Transgression*. München: Fink, c2004.

Shaw, Drew Camppbell. (2004) *Transgression and beyond: Dambudzo Marchera and Zimbabwean literature*. London: University of London, PhD thesis.

Vasse, David. (2004) *Catherine Breillat: un cinéma du rite et de la transgression*. Préface de Catherine Breillat. Bruxelles: Complexe; Issy-les-Moulineaux: Arte.

Chappuzeau, Bernhard. (2005) *Transgression und Trauma bei Pedro Almodóvar und Rainer Werner Fassbinder: Gender-Memoria-Visum*. [Originally presented as the author's doctoral thesis at Universität Düsseldorf].

Craik, Jennifer. (2005) *Uniforms exposed: from conformity to transgression*. Oxford: Berg.

Mergenthaler, Volker. (2005) *Völkerschau–Kannibalismus–Fremdenlegion: zur Ästhetik der Transgression (1897–1936)*. Tübingen: Niemeyer.

Messier, Vartan P. and Nandita Batra, (eds.) (2005) *Transgression and taboo: critical essays*. Mayaguez: CEACC, 2005. [Includes some papers from the conference *Transgression and taboo* held by the CEA-CC in the Spring of 2005].

Miller, James, (ed.) (2005) *Dante & the unorthodox: the aesthetics of transgression.* Waterloo, ON: Wilfrid Laurier University Press.

Mohr, Dunja M. (2005) *Worlds apart? dualism and transgression in contemporary female dystopias.* Jefferson, NC; London: McFarland & Co. [This book was originally handed in as a doctoral thesis at the University of Trier in Germany].

Okun, Kirsten. (2005) *Unbegrenzte Möglichkeiten: Brinkmann- Burroughs- Kerouac: Sexualität, Geschlecht, Körper und Transgression als Subversion dualistischer Denkmuster.* Bielefeld: Aisthesis.

Bolton, Andrew. (2006) *Anglomania: tradition and transgression in British fashion;* introduction by Ian Buruma. New York: The Metropolitan Museum of Art; New Haven, Conn.; London: Yale University Press.

Hussey, Andrew, (ed.) (2006) *The Beast at Heaven's Gate: Georges Bataille and the art of transgression.* Amsterdam: Rodopi.

Jenks, Chris, (ed.) (2006) *Transgression: critical concepts in sociology.* London: Routledge.

Lipka, Hilary B. (2006) *Sexual transgression in the Hebrew Bible.* Sheffield: Phoenix Press.

Monro, Anita. (2006) *Resurrecting erotic transgression: subjecting ambiguity in theology.* London: Equinox Pub. Ltd.

Rao, Ursula and John Hutnyk, eds. (2006) *Celebrating transgression: method and politics in anthropological studies of culture: a book in honour of Klaus Peter Köpping.* New York: Berghahn Books.

Waugh, Thomas. (2006) *The romance of transgression in Canada: queering sexualities, nations, cinemas.* Foreword by Bruce LaBruce. Montreal; London: McGill-Queen's University Press.

Notes

1 Jacques Derrida, *The Ear of the Other*, tr. Peggy Kamuf, ed. Christine MacDonald (Lincoln: University of Nebraska Press, 1985), p. 38.
2 Sandra Harding, *Whose Science? Whose Knowledge? Thinking from Women's Lives* (Milton Keynes: Open University Press, 1991), p. 311.
3 Baudrillard, *Symbolic Exchange and Death*, tr. Iain Hamilton Grant, intro by Mike Gane (London: Sage, 1993), p. 137.
4 Jacques Derrida, 'Faith and Knowledge: the Two Sources of 'Religion' at the Limits of Reason Alone', *Religion*, eds. Jacques Derrida and Gianni Vattimo (Cambridge: Polity Press, 1998), p. 11.
5 Susan Sontag, *Against Interpretation* (London: Vintage, 2001), p. 7.
6 Harding, *Whose Science?*, p. 149.
7 Ibid., p. 150.
8 Pamela Sue Anderson, 'An Epistemological-Ethical Approach to Philosophy of Religion: Learning to Listen', in *Feminist Philosophy of Religion*, eds. Pamela Sue Anderson and Beverley Clack (London and New York: Routledge, 2004), p. 94.
9 Ibid., paraphrasing Michele Le Doeuff, p. 95.
10 Jane Austen, *Persuasion*, ed. Linda Bree (Toronto: Broadview, 2000), p. 69.
11 Mary Wollstonecraft, *A Short Residence in Sweden, Norway and Denmark*, ed. Richard Holmes (Harmondsworth: Penguin, 1987), p. 97.
12 Ibid., p. 158.
13 Janet Todd, 'Thoughts on the Death of Fanny Wollstonecraft', in *Gender, Art and Death* (Oxford; Polity Press, 1993), p. 129.
14 Reproduced in Todd, 'Thoughts on the Death of Fanny Wollstonecraft', p. 129. See, for a full account, Janet Todd's recent book, *Death and the Maidens; Fanny Wollstonecraft and the Shelley Circle* (Profile Books: London, 2007). Vivien Jones's moving piece reflecting on the impact of Wollstonecraft's death on the Anglo-feminist tradition is also recommended: 'The Death of Mary Wollstonecraft', *British Journal for Eighteenth-Century Studies*, 20: 187–205.
15 Linda Grant, 'What Sexual Revolution?', in *Sexuality*, ed. Robert A. Nye (Oxford: Oxford University Press, 1999), p. 360.
16 Ibid., p. 361.
17 Sheila Jeffreys, 'The Sexual Revolution Was for Men', in Nye (ed.), *Sexuality*, p. 362.
18 Georges Bataille, 'The Cruelty of the Inner Self', from *Eroticism*, reproduced in *Sexuality*, ed. Nye, p. 384.
19 Theodor Adorno and Max Horkheimer, *Dialectic of Enlightenment*, tr. John Cumming (London and New York: Verso, 1992), p. 118.

20   Kathy Acker, 'The Words to Say It', in *Bodies of Work: essays by Kathy Acker* (London: Serpent's Tail, 1998), p. 67.

21   Ibid., p. 69.

22   Elizabeth Grosz, 'The Body of Signification', in John Fletcher and Andrew Benjamin (eds.), *Abjection, Melancholia and Love: The Work of Julia Kristeva* (London and New York: Routledge, 1990), p. 98.

23   Iris Young, 'Pregnant Embodiment', in Donn Welton (ed.), *Body and Flesh: A Philosophical Reader* (Oxford: Blackwell, 2001), p. 276. Quoting Julia Kristeva, 'Women's Time'.

24   Young. 'Pregnant Embodiment', p. 276.

25   Changes in care roles have to a certain extent have displaced the latter stages of maternal subjectivity from the biological mother. However, the core human functions of conception, placental function, pregnancy, birth, lactation are specifically functions of female-embodied maternal subjectivity. This is not something that is experienced by everyone, and cannot be discussed in the register of 'gender equality', but it is arguably the *universal* ground or foundation of human subjectivity.

26   Jane Spencer, 'Afterword: Feminist Waves', in *Third Wave Feminism*, 2nd edition, eds. Stacy Gillis, Gillian Howie and Rebecca Munford (Basingstoke: Palgrave Macmillan, 2007), p. 299.

27   Suzanne Guerlac, 'Bataille in Theory: Afterimages (Lascaux)', *Diacritics: a review of contemporary criticism*, (Summer 1996) 26:2, pp. 6–7.

28   Unpublished final paragraph edited out of his introduction to *Eroticism*, tr. Mary Dalwood (Harmondsowrth: Penguin, 2001).

29   Georges Bataille, 'Madame Edwarda', tr. Austryn Wainhouse (London and New York: Marion Books, 2003), p. 150.

30   Judith Butler, (1990) *Gender Trouble: Feminism and the Subversion of Identity*, New York and London: Routledge, p. 64: 'In melancholia, the loved object is lost through a variety of means: separation, death, or the breaking of an emotional tie. In the Oedipal situation, however, the loss is dictated by a *prohibition* attended by a set of punishments. The melancholia of gender identification which 'answers' the Oedipal dilemma must be understood, then, as the internalization of an interior moral directive which gains its structure and energy from an externally enforced taboo. Although Freud does not explicitly argue in its favour, it would appear that the taboo against homosexuality must *precede* the heterosexual incest taboo; the taboo against homosexuality in effect creates the heterosexual 'dispositions' by which the Oedipal conflict becomes possible. The young boy and young girl who enter into the Oedipal drama with incestuous heterosexual aims have already been subjected to prohibitions which 'dispose' them in distinct sexual directions. Hence, the dispositions that Freud assumes to be primary or constitutive facts of sexual life are effects of a law which, internalized, produces and regulated discrete gender identity and heterosexuality.'

31   Bataille, *Eroticism*, p. 15.

32   Ibid., p. 22.

33   By 'we' here I am calling on a community of thinkers who recognize the thoughts I aim to follow to an as yet unexplored conclusion. If you

recognize something of what I am thinking, feel free to follow and consider that conclusion. If you do not recognize anything in this, are not excited by transgressive thoughts, or if you are excited by their distorted manifestation in other orders of transgressive social actions (such as exorbitating eyes or ingesting bull's testicles) perhaps it's best to read something else today.

34 Denis Hollier, *Against Architecture: The Writings of Georges Bataille* (Cambridge, Massachusetts: MIT Press, 1992), p. 24.

35 Ibid., p. 150.

36 Anthony Julius, *Transgressions: The Offences of Art* (London: Thames and Hudson, 2002), p. 10.

37 Ibid., pp. 16–17.

38 Ibid., pp. 19–20.

39 Ibid., p. 22.

40 Georges Bataille, *Story of the Eye* (Harmondsworth: Penguin, 2001), p. 67.

41 Michel Foucault, 'Preface to Transgression', in *Language, Counter-memory, Practice: selected essays and interviews*, trans. D.F.B. and Sherry Simone, ed. Donald F. Bouchard (Oxford: Blackwell, 1977), pp. 46–7.

42 Bataille, *Eroticism*, pp. 21–2.

43 Georges Bataille, 'The Psychological Structure of Fascism', in *The Bataille Reader*, ed. Fred Botting and Scott Wilson (Oxford: Blackwell, 2000), p. 145.

44 Michael Richardson, *Georges Bataille* (London and New York: Routledge, 1994), p. 93.

45 Kathy Acker, 'Critical languages', in *Bodies of Work: essays by Kathy Acker* (Lonond: Serpent's tail, 1997), p. 89, 91.

46 Michel Surya, *Georges Bataille: an intellectual biography*, tr. Krzysztof Fijalkowski and Michael Richardson (London and New York: Verso, 2002), p. 260. This translation of Surya's fascinating biography of Bataille has shaped and informed my understanding of the personal context for his work. It is a remarkable book.

47 Bataille, 'The Meaning of General Economy', in *The Bataille Reader*, p. 184.

48 Bataille, 'The Object of Desire and the Totality of the Real', in *The Bataille Reader*, p. 270.

49 John Keats, 'Ode to a Grecian Urn' (1819). I am thinking through the terms of Helen Vendler's compelling account of the 'Grecian Urn' as a study of 'sexual pursuit and flight, of music-making and courtship, and of communal religious performance', in *The Odes of John Keats* (Cambridrge, Mass.: Harvard University Press, 1983), pp. 114–5, p. 117.

50 A. C. Graylong, *Against All Gods: six polemics on religion and an essay on kindness* (London: Oberon Books, 2007), p. 42.

51 Ibid., p. 10.

52 Ibid., p. 47.

53 Sandra Harding, *Whose Science? Whose Knowledge? Thinking from women's lives* (Milton Keynes: Open University Press, 1991).

54 Bataille, 'The Sorcerer's Apprentice', in *Visions of Excess: selected writings, 1927–1939*, tr. Allan Stoekl with Carl R. Lovitt and Donald M. Leslie Jr.,

ed. Allan Stoekl (Minneapolis: University of Minnesota Press, 2004), p. 226, 227.

55 Foucault, 'Preface to Transgression', pp. 59–60.

56 Bataille, 'The Object of Desire and the Totality of the Real', in *The Bataille Reader*, p. 264, 267.

57 Fred Botting and Scott Wilson (eds), introduction to *Bataille: A Critical Reader* (Oxford: Blackwell, 1998), p. 7.

58 Bataille, 'The Sorcerer's Apprentice', p. 229.

59 Bataille, 'Le Coupable: Found fragments on Laure', in *Laure: The collected writings*, tr. Jeanine Herman (San Francisco: City Lights Books, 1995), p. 254–5.

60 Quoted by Surya, *Georges Bataille*, p. 26.

61 Ibid., p. 52.

62 Ibid., p. 83.

63 Bataille, 'Autobiographical Note', in *Laure*, p. 217.

64 Bataille quoted by Surya, *Georges Bataille*, p. 353.

65 Bataille, 'The Object of Desire and the Totality of the Real', in *The Bataille Reader*, p. 267.

66 Ibid., p. 256.

67 Sheri I. Hoem, 'Community and the "Absolutely Feminine" ', *Diacritics: a review of contemporary criticism*, (Summer 1996) 26:2, p. 56.

68 Bataille, 'The Object of Desire and the Totality of the Real', p. 269.

69 Slavoj Žižek, *The Parallax View* (Cambridge, Mass.: The MIT Press, 2006), p. 95. And see Surya, p. 451.

70 Bataille', 'Preface' to *Madame Edwarda*, in *My Mother Madame Edwarda The Dead Man*, tr. Austryn Wainhouse (London and New York: Marion Boyars, 2003), p. 138.

71 Surya, p. 572.

72 Fred Botting and Scott Wilson, *Bataille* (Basingstoke: Palgrave, 2001), p. 87. See also Elisabeth Roudinesco, *Jacques Lacan*, trans. Barbara Bray (Cambridge: Polity press, 1997).

73 Bataille, *Eroticism*, p. 109.

74 Žižek, *Parallax View*, p. 95.

75 A difficult example of sexuality as primary transgression for Foucault is documented in *History of Sexuality, vol 1* [1976]: the 'farm hand ... who was somewhat simple-minded' obtained 'a few caresses from a little girl, just as he had done before and seen done by the village urchins round about him' in a game called 'curdled milk'. The farm hand was indicted and subject to a published report. The 'significant thing about this story' for Foucault is its 'pettiness', 'the fact that this everyday occurrence in the life of village sexuality, these inconsequential bucolic pleasures, could become, from a certain time, the object not only of a collective intolerance but of a judicial action, a medical intervention, a careful criminal examination, and an entire theoretical elaboration'. These 'timeless gestures, these barely furtive pleasures between simple-minded adults and alert children' became for Foucault 'a whole machinery for speechifying, analyzing, and investigating.' (Foucault 1990, 31–2) What is at stake in this anecdote? James Miller also notes that

in a 'public conversation' Foucault had argued that 'in no circumstances should sexuality be subject to any kind of legislation whatsoever'. *The Passion of Michel Foucault* (London: Harper Collins, 1993), p. 257.

76   Roland Barthes, 'The Metaphor of the Eye', tr. J. A. Underwood, in Bataille, *Story of the Eye* (Harmondsworth: Penguin, 2001), p. 125.

77   Ibid., p. 122.

78   Ibid., p. 124.

79   Bataille, 'Coincidences', in *Story of the Eye*, p. 73.

80   Ibid., p. 72.

81   This is the one point on which Bataille's biographer, Michel Surya, seems actually shaken by his subject: 'Bataille twice presented this outrage as being real . . . he incorporated it into a story, *Blue of Noon*, which there can be no doubt, unlike *Story of the Eye*, is in large part indebted to autobiographical elements . . . This (if it is real) calls for comment, less to diminish its obscenity than to accompany it with its most extreme reasons: what springs up from transgression is located beyond the scandalous, at the same time as it belongs to it entirely' (Surya, 150–1).

82   Julia Kristeva, 'Postmodernism?', in *Modernism/Postmodernism*, ed. Peter Brooker (Essex: Longman, 1992), p. 201.

83   Yukio Mishima, 'Georges Bataille and Divinus Deus', in Georges Bataille, *My Mother Madame Edwarda The Dead Man*, tr. Austryn Wainhouse with essays by Yukio Mishima and Ken Hollings (London and New York: Marion Boyars, 2003), p. 14.

84   Nick Land, *The Thirst for Annihilation: Georges Bataille and Virulent Nihilism (an essay on atheistic religion)* (London and New York: Routledge, 1992), p. 89.

85   Michel Houellebecq, *The Possibility of an Island*, tr. Gavin Bowd (London: Phoenix, 2006), p. 14.

86   An interesting memory illuminates this point: 'One night, we were awakened, my mother and I, by vehement words that the syphilitic was literally howling in his room: he had suddenly gone mad. I went for the doctor, who came immediately . . . The doctor had withdrawn to the next room with my mother and I had remained with the blind lunatic, when he shrieked in a stentorian voice: "Doctor, let me know when you're done fucking my wife!" For me, that utterance, which in a split second annihilated the demoralizing effects of a strict upbringing, left me with something like a steady obligation, unconscious and unwilled: the necessity of finding an equivalent to that sentence in any situation I happen to be in; and this largely explains *Story of the Eye*' (Bataille, 'Coincidences', p. 73).

87   Susan Rubin-Suleiman, *Subversive Intent: Gender, Politics and the Avant-Garde* (Cambridge: Harvard University Press, 1990), pp. 86–7.

88   Denis Hollier, *Against Architecture: the writings of Georges Bataille*, tr. Betsy Wing (Cambridge, Mass.: MIT Press, 1992), p. 109.

89   Ibid., p. 15.

90   Bataille, *Eroticism*, p. 21.

91   Jean-François Lyotard. *Libidinal Economy*, tr. Iain Hamilton Grant (London: Continuum, 2004), p. 133.

92   Ibid., p. 135.
93   Ibid., p. 135, 136.
94   Ibid., p. 137, 138.
95   Botting and Wilson, introduction to *Bataille: A Critical Reader* (Oxford: Blackwell, 1998), p. 16.
96   Gillian Howie, 'Interview with Luce Irigaray', in *Third Wave Feminism: A Critical Exploration*, 2nd edition (Houndmills: Palgrave Macmillan, 2007), p. 288.
97   Colette Peignot, 'Correspondence', in *Laure*, p. 152.
98   Ibid., p. 238.
99   Simone Weil, *Oppression and Liberty*, tr. Arthur Wills and John Petrie (London and New York: Routledge, 2001), p. 181.
100 Peignot, 'Political Texts', in *Laure*, p. 213.
101 Ibid., p. 203.
102 Milo Sweedler, 'From the Sacred Conspiracy to the Unavowable Community: Bataille, Blanchot and Laure's *Le Sacré*, *French Studies* (2005) 59:3, pp. 339–40.
103 Ibid., pp. 340–1.
104 Bataille, *Eroticism*, p. 17.
105 Ibid., p. 18, 20.
106 Sweedler, 'From the Sacred Conspiracy to the Unavowable Community', p. 347.
107 Bataille, 'Le Coupable', in *Laure*, p. 262.
108 Chris Jenks, *Transgression* (London and New York: Routledge, 2003), p. 88.
109 Quoted by Fred Botting and Scott Wilson, introduction to *Bataille: A Critical Reader* (Oxford: Blackwell, 1998), p. 8.
110 Jenks, *Transgression*, p. 69, 81.
111 Ibid., pp. 89–90.
112 Ibid., p. 92.
113 Ibid., p. 98.
114 Bataille, 'The Sacred', in *Visions of Excess*, p. 241.
115 Michèle Roberts, (2005) 'The Return' in *The New Poetry*, ed. Michael Hulse, David Kennedy and David Morley. Tarset: Bloodaxe Books, p. 150.
116 Hoem, 'Community and the Absolutely Feminine', p. 55.
117 Foucault, 'Preface to Transgression', p. 33.
118 Botting and Wilson, *Bataille: A Critical Reader*, p. 2.
119 Bataille, 'The Sorcerer's Apprentice', p. 228.
120 Bataille, *Eroticism*, p. 17.
121 Judith Starkis, 'No fun and games until someone loses an eye: transgression and masculinity in Bataille and Foucault', *Diacritics: a review of contemporary criticism* (Summer 1996) 26:2, p. 20.
122 Bataille, *Eroticism*, pp. 38–9.
123 Ibid., p. 23.
124 Ibid., pp. 23–4.
125 Ibid., p. 25.
126 Ibid., pp. 13–14.

127   Maryline Lukacher, *Maternal Fictions: Stendhal, Sand, Rachilde, and Bataille* (Durham and London: Duke University Press, 1994), p. 171.

128   Julia Kristeva in interview, quoted by Lydia Rainford, *She Changes by Intrigue: Irony, Femininity and Feminism* (Amsterdam and New York: Rodopi, 2005), p. 22, n. 5.

129   Iris Marion Young, 'Pregnant Embodiment', in Donn Welton (ed.), *Body and Flesh: A Philosophical Reader* (Oxford: Blackwell, 1998), p. 280.

130   Janet Martin Soskice, 'Love and Attention', in *Feminist Philosophy of Religion*, ed. Pamela Sue Anderson and Beverley Clack (London and New York: Routledge, 2004), p. 207.

131   Starkis, 'No fun and games until someone loses an eye', p. 19.

132   Ibid., p. 20, 23.

133   Ibid., p. 30.

134   Guerlac, 'Bataille in Theory', p. 7.

135   Peignot, 'Story of Donald', in *Laure*, p. 179.

136   If you have never read *Story of O* I strongly recommend you experience that before this. In fact, if you have read neither *Story of the Eye* nor *Story of O* you will find this discussion inexplicably strange. Watch out though, the material I am discussing here is strong, not so much in the sense of shocking, as in the sense of violently and involuntarily affective. Visceral nausea is the primary reaction I now experience to reading (and writing about) *Story of the Eye*; *Story of O* is equally difficult – for different reasons – to read and to write about with any sustained coherence.

137   See Jérôme Peignot, 'My Diagonal Mother', in *Laure*, pp. 296–7; Surya, p. 266.

138   Surya, *Georges Bartaille*, p. 568.

139   Jean Paulhan, 'A Slave's Revolt: an essay on *The Story of O*', in Pauline Réage (London: Corgi Books, 1994), pp. 272–3.

140   Réage, *Story of O*, p. 253.

141   Susan Sontag, 'The Pornographic Imagination', in Bataille, *Story of the Eye*, p. 94.

142   Ibid., p. 99.

143   Ibid., p. 127.

144   Ibid., pp. 47–8.

145   Ibid., p. 17.

146   Ibid., p. 57.

147   Ibid., p. 64.

148   Ibid., p. 130.

149   Sontag, 'Pornographic Imagination', p. 102.

150   Ibid., p. 102.

151   Anne Carolyn Klein, 'Finding a Self: Buddhist and Feminist Perspectives', in *Philosophy of Religion: An Anthology*, eds Charles Taliaferro and Paul J. Griffiths (Oxford: Blackwell, 2003), p. 331.

152   Réage, *Story of O*, pp. 154–5.

153   Ibid., p. 263.

154   Bataille, 'Letter to X, Lecturer on Hegel', *The Bataille Reader*, p. 299.

155   Ted Honderich (ed.), *The Oxford Companion to Philosophy* (Oxford: Oxford University Press, 1995), pp. 638.

156   Austen, *Persuasion*, p. 244.

157   Réage, *Story of O*, p. 253.

158   Sontag, 'Pornographic Imagination', p. 115.

159   William Blake, letter to Revd Dr Trusler, 23 August 1799, in *Romanticism: an anthology*, ed. Duncan Wu (Oxford: Blackwell, 1994), pp. 107–8: 'I feel that a man may be happy in this world. And I know that this world is a world of imagination and vision. I see everything I paint in this world, but everybody does not see alike. To the eyes of a miser, a guinea is more beautiful than the sun, and a bag worn with the use of money has more beautiful proportions than a vine filled with grapes. The tree which moves some to tears of joy is, in the eyes of others, only a green thing that stands in the way. Some see nature all ridicule and deformity (and by these I shall not regulate my proportions), and some scarce see nature at all. But to the eyes of the man of imagination, nature is imagination itself. As a man is so he sees; as the eye is formed, such are its powers.'

160   Bataille, 'Notre-Dame de Rhiems' [1918], reproduced in Hollier, *Against Architecture*, p. 19.

161   C.S. Lewis, *Surprised by Joy: The Shape of My Early Life* [1935] (London and Glasgow: Fontana, 1973), p. 179.

162   Paul Hegarty, *Georges Bataille: Core Cultural Theorist* (London: Sage, 2000), p. 124.

163   Foucault, 'Preface to Transgression', p. 30. Quoted by Hegarty, p. 124.

164   Ibid., p. 32.

165   Ibid., pp. 29–30.

166   Philippe Sollers, 'The Roof: Essay in Systematic Reading', in Fred Botting and Scott Wilson (eds), *Bataille: A Critical Reader* (Oxford: Blackwell, 1998), p. 75.

167   Ibid., p. 77.

168   Bataille quoted by Sollers, 'The Roof', p. 79.

169   Lyotard quoted by Botting and Wilson, *Bataille*, p. 15.

170   Jenks, *Transgression*, p. 89.

171   Catherine Townsend, *Sleeping Around: Secrets of a Sexual Adventuress* (London: John Murray, 2007), p. 3.

172   Ibid., p. 110.

173   *Sunday Times*, 20 August 2006, p. 2.

174   Bataille, *Eroticism*, p. 111.

175   Millet, *The Sexual Life of Catherine M*, p. 32, 33.

176   Friedrich Nietzsche, *The Gay Science*, quoted by Land, *Thirst for Annihilation*, p. 85.

177   Percy Bysshe Shelly, 'The Necessity of Atheism', *The Works of Percy Bysshe Shelley*, eds Roger Ingpen and Walter E. Peck, Volume V (New York: Charles Scribener's Sons, 1928), p. 289.

178   Marquis de Sade quoted by Nick Land, *Thirst for Annihilation*, p. 62.

179   Land, *Thirst for Annihilation*, p. 78.

180   Ibid., p. 20.

181   Bataille, 'Guilty', in *The Bataille Reader*, p. 10.

182   William Blake, 'The Divine Image', *Songs of Innocence and of Experience: shewing the two contrary states of the human soul* [1789–1794] (Oxford: Oxford University Press, 1970), plate 18.

183 Sir Geoffrey Keynes' comments on this poem are interesting: 'It can be interpreted as providing the disillusioning discovery that human nature in its most evil moments can exhibit the very opposite of the attributes described in *Innocence*. It is possible that the poem was designed as a late edition or alternative theme for *Experience*, written perhaps during a violent revulsion of feeling produced by the war with France.' (Ibid., p. 125.)

184 Sollers, 'The Roof', p. 75.

185 James Frazer, *The Golden Bough: a History of Myth and Religion* (London: Macmillan, 1994), p. 539.

186 Ibid., p. 300.

187 Land, *Thirst for Annihilation*, p. 75.

188 *London Review of Books* 28:20 (19 October 2006). Accessed online, 28.03.07: http://www.lrb.co.uk/v28/n20/, page 3 of 6.

189 Karen Armstrong, *A History of God. From Abraham to the Present: the 4000-year Quest for God* (London: Vintage, 1993), p. 10.

190 Ibid., p. 363.

191 C.S. Lewis, *The Four Loves* [1962] (London: Harper Collins, 2002), p. 124.

192 Perhaps only Marx, Freud and Darwin have produced writing that has forced a *material* change in the configuration of the world, and this was not fiction or poetry. It depends what you mean by change though. Austen changed the nature of female subjectivity; the interiority of being female shifted in the English tradition following the popular reception of Austen's English *realism*.

193 Michel Houellebecq, *Atomised* (London: Vintage Books, 2001), p. 376–7.

194 Bataille, 'The Accursed Share', in *The Bataille Reader*, p. 261.

195 Bataille, *Literature and Evil* [1957], tr. Alastair Hamilton (London: Calder and Boyars, 1973).

196 C.S. Lewis, 'Christianity and Literature' [1940], in *Christian Reflections*, ed. Walter Hooper (Glasgow: Collins, 1980), p. 17.

197 Rosemary Jackson, *Fantasy: the literature of subversion* (London and New York: Methuen, 1981), p. 140.

198 Ibid., p. 153.

199 Ibid., p. 154.

200 Ibid., p. 155.

201 Tom Shippey, *J.R.R. Tolkien: Author of the Century* (London: Harper Collins, 2000), pp. xx–xxi.

202 A more recent poll of the favourite 'Love Story' voted Bronte's *Wuthering Heights* first.

203 Ibid., p. 308.

204 Ibid., p. viii.

205 Ibid., p. ix.

206 Bataille, 'Le Coupable', in *Laure*, p. 257.

207 Lewis, *Atlantic Monthly* 1959, quoted by A. N. Wilson, *C. S. Lewis: a biography* (London: Collins, 1990), p. 278.

208 Wilson, *C. S. Lewis*, p. 251.

209 Ibid., p. 128.

210 Ibid., p. 224.

211   Lewis, *Allegory of Love: a study in Medieval tradition* (Oxford: Oxford University Press, 1970), p. 7.
212   Lewis, *Surprised by Joy*, p. 21.
213   C.S. Lewis, *The Lion, The Witch and the Wardrobe* (London: Collins, 1998), pp. 12–13.
214   Bataille, *Story of the Eye*, p. 17.
215   Ibid., p. 17.
216   Quoted by Shippey, *J.R.R. Tolkien*, p. xxii.
217   Tolkien, 'Tree and Leaf', in *Tree and Leaf, including the Poem Mythopoeia, The Homecoming of BEORHTNOTH* (London: Harper Collins, 2001), p. 58.
218   C.S. Lewis, *Surprised by Joy: The Shape of My Early Life* [1935] (London and Glasgow: Fontana, 1973), p. 139.
219   Lewis, 'Christianity and Literature', p. 25.
220   Lewis, *The Screwtape Letters* (London: Harper Collins, 2002), pp. 31–2.
221   Tolkien, 'Tree and Leaf', p. 58.
222   Jackson, *Fantasy*, p. 155.
223   Ibid., pp. 155–6.
224   Tolkien, 'On Fairy-Stories' [1939], in *Essays Presented to Charles Williams* (Michigan: William B. Eerdmans Publishing, 1973), p. 50.
225   Ibid., p. 58.
226   Gillian Howie, 'Interview with Luce Irigaray', in *Third Wave Feminism*, 2nd edition, eds Stacy Gillis, Gillian Howie and Rebecca Munford (Basingstoke: Palgrave Macmillan, 2007), p. 283.
227   Tolkien, 'On Fairy-Stories', p. 56.
228   Bataille, 'The Sorcerer's Apprentice', p. 233.
229   Ibid., p. 232.
230   Lewis, *The Four Loves* (London: Harper Vollins, 2002), pp. 113–4.
231   Bataille, 'The Accursed Share', in *The Bataille Reader*, p. 261.
232   Lewis, *The Lion, The Witch and the Wardrobe*, p. 143.
233   Lewis, *Four Loves*, p. 170.
234   Darko Suvin, 'Inside the Whale, or *etsi communismus non dareteur*: reflections on how to live when a truly just society is a necessity but nowhere on the horizon', *Critical Quarterly* (Spring 2007) 49:1, p. 129.
235   Lewis, *Surprised by Joy*, pp. 182–3.
236   Ibid., p. 183.
237   Lewis, *The Four Loves*, pp. 113–4.
238   Ibid., p. 179.
239   Bataille, 'The Sacred', p. 232.
240   Tolkien, 'On Fairy Stories', p. 69.
241   Ibid., p. 69.
242   Bataille, 'Preface' to *Madame Edwarda*, p. 142.
243   Lewis, *Four Loves*, p. 126.
244   Lewis, 'That Hideous Strength', in *The Cosmic Trilogy* [1938–1945] (London: The Bodley Head, 1990), p. 589.
245   Ibid., p. 590.
246   Ibid., p. 647.
246   Ibid., p. 649.

248 Northrop Frye, *Words With Power: being a second study of the Bible and Literature* (San Diego: Harcourt Brace Jovanovich, 1990), p. 201.

249 Ibid., p. 192.

250 Ibid., p. 218.

251 Howie, 'Interview with Luce Irigaray', p. 290.

252 C.S. Lewis, *Collected Letters*, Vol. 1: Family Letters 1905–1931, ed. Walter Hooper (London: Harper Collins, 2000), p. 269.

253 Ibid., p. 274.

254 Ibid., p. 313.

255 Ibid., pp. 877–8.

256 Lewis, 'That Hideous Strength', p. 641.

257 Lewis, 'That Hideous Strength', p. 487.

258 Ibid., p. 624.

259 Bataille, *Eroticism*, p. 206.

260 Bataille, 'Coupable', in *Laure*, p. 273.

261 Lewis, *A Grief Observed* (London: Faber and Faber, 1966), pp. 5–6.

262 Ibid., p. 25.

263 Ibid., p. 22.

264 Ibid., p. 26.

265 Ibid., pp. 35, 37–8.

266 Marcella Althaus-Reid, *From Feminist Theology to Indecent Theology* (London: SCM Press, 2004), p. 175.

267 Lewis, 'The Poison of Subjectivism', in *Christian Reflections* (Glasgow: Collins, 1980), p. 102.

268 If there are, as Chris Jenks has observed following the logic of transgressive thought, no rule of law that should not be transgressed, then what has prevented me from plagiarizing his published work?

269 Ibid., pp. 108–9.

270 Lewis, 'The Poison of Subjectivism', p. 102.

271 Lewis, 'Perelandra', in *The Cosmic Trilogy*, p. 180.

272 Peignot, 'Story of Donald', in *Laure*, p. 179.

273 Land, *Thirst for Annihilation*, p. xix.

274 Peignot, 'Political Texts', in *Laure*, p. 211.

275 Kathy Acker, 'The Words to Say It', in *Bodies of Work*, p. 69.

276 Joy Davidman, 'This Woman', *Letter to a Comrade*, ed. Stephen Vincent Benet (New Haven: Yale University Press, 1938), p. 54.

277 Sontag, 'Piety Without Content', in *Against Interpretation*, p. 249.

278 Acker, 'Seeing Gender', in *Bodies of Work*, p. 158.

279 Acker, 'Critical Languages', in *Bodies of Work*, p. 90.

280 Ibid., p. 91.

281 Ibid., p. 91.

282 Ibid., p. 92.

283 Ibid., p. 97.

284 Acker, 'Writing, Identity, and Copyright in the Net Age', in *Bodies of Work*, p. 98.

285 Acker, 'Seeing Gender', p. 160; Judith Butler, 'Bodies that Matter,' in *Engaging With Irigaray: Feminist Philosophy and Modern European Thought*,

eds Carolyn Burke, Naomi Schor and Margaret Whitford (New York: Columbia University Press, 1994), p. 143.

286   Sontag, 'Piety Without Content', p. 249.

287   Bataille, *Eroticism*, p. 36.

288   Ibid., p. 37.

289   Ibid., p. 38.

290   Sontag, 'The Artist as Exemplary Sufferer', in *Against Interpretation*, p. 47.

291   Ibid., p. 48.

292   Sontag, 'Simone Weil', in *Against Interpretation*, p. 49, 50.

293   Ibid., p. 50.

294   Sontag, *Against Interpretation*, p. 262.

295   Luce Irigaray, *The Way of Love*, tr. Heidi Bostic and Stephen Pluháček (London and New York: Continuum, 2002), p. 172.

296   Colette Peignot, 'Story of Donald', in *Laure*, p. 179.

297   Sontag, 'Simone Weil', in *Against Interpretation*, p. 51.

298   Catherine Millet, *The Sexual Life of Catherine M* (London: Corgi, 2003), p. 251.

299   Catherine Townsend, *Sleeping Around*, p. 3.

300   Ibid., p. 63.

301   Millet, *The Sexual Life of Catherine M*, p. 20.

302   Ibid., p. 154.

303   Ibid., p. 52, 55.

304   Ibid., p. 120, 118.

305   Ibid., p. 53.

306   Ibid., p. 73.

307   Ibid., p. 68.

308   Catherine Millet, *The Sexual Life of Catherine M*, p. 81.

309   Bataille, *Eroticism*, p. 131.

310   Millet, *The Sexual Life of Catherine M*, p. 96.

311   Jane Austen, *Pride and Prejudice* [1813], ed. Robert P. Irvine (Ontario: Broadview, 2002), p. 259.

312   Wolfgang Iser, *How to Do Theory* (Oxford: Blackwell, 2006), p. 5.

313   Bataille, 'The Sacred Conspiracy', in *Visions of Excess*, p. 179.

314   Iser, *How to Do Theory*, p. 6.

315   Michael Richardson, *Georges Bataille* (New York & London: Routledge, 1994), p. 102; Jenks, *Transgression*, p. 69.

316   Richardson, *Georges Bataille*, p. 6.

317   Lawrence R. Schehr, 'Lyotard's Codpiece', *in Yale French Studies*, 99 (2001), p. 72.

318   Colette Peignot, 'Notes on the Revolution', in *Laure*, p. 226.

319   Acker, 'Seeing Gender', p. 161.

320   Acker, 'Seeing Gender', p. 166.

321   Millet, *The Sexual Life of Catherine M*, p. 137.

322   Maryline Lukacher, *Maternal Fictions: Stendhal, Sand, Rachilde, and Bataille* (Durham and London: Duke University Press, 1994), pp. 180–1.

323   Ibid., p. 180.

324   Bataille, quoted by Lukacher, *Maternal Fictions*, p. 179.

325   Adorno and Horkheimer, *Dialectic of Enlightenment*, p. 244.

326   Lewis, 'The Poison of Subjectivism', p. 126.

327 Herbert Marcuse, 'Eros and Human Emancipation', in *Sexuality*, ed. Robert A. Nye (Oxford; Oxford University Press, 1999), p. 127.

328 Ibid., p. 351.

329 Marcuse, 'Eros and Human Emancipation', p. 351.

330 Adorno and Horkheimer, *Dialectic of Enlightenment*, p. 204.

331 Howie, 'Interview with Luce Irigaray', p. 285.

332 Schehr, 'Lyotard's Codpiece', p. 68, 73, 76.

333 Lukacher, *Maternal Fictions*, p. 180. See also Jane Gallop, 'Sade, Mothers and other Women', in *Sade and the Narrative of Transgression*, ed. David B. Allison, Mark S. Roberts and Allen S. Weiss (Cambridge; Cambridge University Press, 1995), pp. 122–141.

334 Millet, *Sexual Life*, p. 36.

335 Acker, 'The Words to Say It', in *Bodies of Work*, p. 69.

336 Adorno and Horkheimer, *Dialectic of Enlightenment*, pp. 101–2.

337 Angela Carter, *The Sadean Woman: an exercise in cultural history* (London: Virago, 1979), p. 147.

338 Ibid., p. 147.

339 Surya, *Georges Bataille*, p. 386.

340 Editor's introduction to Yuasa Yasuo, *The Body: toward an Eastern mind-body theory*, ed. T. P. Kasulis, tr. By Nagatomo Shigenori and T. P. Kasulis (New York: State University of New York Press, 1987), p. 3.

341 Miller, *The Passion of Michel Foucault*, p. 31.

342 Ibid., p. 251.

343 Carter, *Sadean Woman*, p. 147.

344 Nick Hocking, 'Bataille's Transgression and Buddhist Tantra: Sex, Style and Spirituality, University of Exeter Undergraduate Dissertation 2006, p. 1.

345 Bataille, 'The Sacred', pp. 240–1.

346 Klein, 'Finding a Self', p. 338.

347 Carter, *Sadean Woman*, p. 150.

348 Bataille, *Eroticism*, p. 16.

349 Tsong-Kha-Pa, *The Great Treatise on the Stages of the Path to Enlightenment* [1402], vol. 2. Translated by The Lamrim Chenmo Translation Committee: Editor in Chief, Joshua W. C. Cutler; Editor, Guy Newland (Ithaca, New York: Snow Lion Publications, 2004), p. 41.

350 Klein, 'Finding a Self', p. 337.

351 Klein, 'Finding a Self', p. 337.

352 Tsong-Kha-Pa, *Great Treatise*, p. 54.

353 Ibid., p. 54.

354 Jamie Morgan, 'Ontological Causistry? Bhaskar's Meta-Reality, Fine Strucuture, and Human Disposition', *Critical Realism Today*, 56 (Autumn 2005), p. 137.

355 Dean, Jospeh and Norrie (eds), 'Editorial', *Critical Realism Today*, pp. 17–18.

356 Irigaray, *The Way of Love*, p. 159.

357 SlavojŽižek, *The Parallax View*, p. 384.

358 Acker, 'Seeing Gender', op. cit., p. 166.

359 Joy Davidman, 'Prayer Against Barrenness', in *Letter to a Comrade*, p. 61.

Index